SEVEN FRESH WINESKINS

Daily readings from the
Old Testament

Also available:

William Barclay: the authorized biography by Clive L Rawlins
ISBN 0 85364 392 X
Ever yours: a selection from the letters of William Barclay,
compiled and edited by Clive L Rawlins
ISBN 0 948095 04 0
A man and his music: Arthur Montford talks to William Barclay
(cassette)
ISBN 0 948095 02 4

SEVEN FRESH WINESKINS

Daily readings from the
Old Testament

William Barclay, CBE DD

LABARUM PUBLICATIONS LTD
DUNBAR

First published 1985 by Labarum Publications Ltd
The Abbey, Dunbar, East Lothian, Scotland

ISBN 0 948095 05 9
    British Library Cataloguing in Publication Data
Barclay, William, *1907-1978*
    Seven fresh wineskins: daily readings from
    the Old Testament.
    1. Bible. O.T. — Commentaries
    I. Title
    221.6 BS1171.2
    ISBN 0-948095-05-9

Printed in Great Britain by
Clark Constable, Edinburgh, London, Melbourne

Jesus said,
"New wine is not put into old wineskins; if it is, the skins burst, and the wine is spilled, and the skins are destroyed ... new wine is put into fresh wineskins, and so both are preserved."

(Matthew 9:17)

PUBLISHER'S NOTE

These meditations were first published shortly after the last war, and reflect the issues then uppermost in William Barclay's mind, as well as the current manner of expressing them.

For the next thirty years he was at pains to develop his views and state them more plainly. During this time he nurtured the hope of writing more expansively on the Old Testament, but never found the opportunity to do so. Because of his high regard for the Old Testament as part of the Word of God, it is fitting that this selection should be made available.

We are grateful to the trustees of the William Barclay Estate for their permission to offer *Seven fresh wineskins* to you, and to the International Bible Reading Society who kindly made the original material available.

CONTENTS

THE BEGINNING OF THE STORY

GENESIS

In these meditations we shall go back to the beginnings of things. We shall see how behind all things there is the creating power of God, who made all things and made them well. Then we shall see how men in their folly blotted and marred the fair face of the earth. And yet, in his great goodness, God did not completely destroy the world that his hands had made.

In the life of Abraham, we shall see how God chose a man who should be the founder of a people, through whom his purposes could be worked out. In the life of Jacob and Isaac, and Joseph, God's guiding hand will be evident still.

Two thoughts must be in our minds. First, the creation of God. 'The earth is the Lord's and the fulness thereof.' This is God's world because behind it is his power. And second, we must be thinking of the providence of God. Behind everything there is the unfolding purpose of God working through the lives of men.

As we think of these things, let us commit ourselves afresh to the love and power of our God.

IN THE BEGINNING GOD

Genesis 1:1-5

¹In the beginning God created the heavens and the earth. ²The earth was without form and void, and darkness was upon the face of the deep; and the Spirit of God was moving over the face of the waters.

³And God said, "Let there be light"; and there was light. ⁴And God saw that the light was good; and God separated the light from the darkness. ⁵God called the light Day, and the darkness he called Night.

In every new beginning there should be God.

(i) We should begin each day with God. We should ever go out to the presence of men from the presence of God. If we do no more we should at least pray Sir Jacob Astley's prayer, 'Lord, Thou Knowest how busy I shall be this day: if I forget Thee, do not Thou forget me.'

(ii) We should begin each week with God. A little girl said that she always saw the days of the week in her imagination as carriages of a train and Sunday was the engine. If we begin the week in the house of God and in the presence of God it will give us strength and grace to get through it.

(iii) We should begin each enterprise with God. When we make plans to do this or that we should offer them to God so that we may be certain that we are following not our will but his. If we do that then for us also there shall be light.

A prayer: *O God, help us never to begin anything without you.*

GOD SAW THAT IT WAS GOOD

Genesis 1:6-12

⁶And God said, "Let there be a firmament in the midst of the waters, and let it separate the waters from the waters." ⁷And God made the firmament and separated the waters which were under the firmament from the waters which were above the firmament. And it was so. ⁸And God called the firmament Heaven. And there was evening and there was morning, a second day.

⁹And God said, "Let the waters under the heavens be gathered together into one place, and let the dry land appear." And it was so. ¹⁰God called the dry land Earth, and the waters that were gathered together he called Seas. And God saw that it was good. ¹¹And God said, "Let the earth put forth vegetation, plants yielding seed, and fruit trees bearing fruit in which is their seed, each according to its kind, upon the earth." And it was so. ¹²The earth brought forth vegetation, plants yielding seed according to their own kinds, and trees bearing fruit in which is their seed, each according to its kind. And God saw that it was good.

God's world is a lovely world. An old Scotsman used to slip away to the hillside after breakfast every morning. People wondered why he went and one day someone asked him. "I go out to the hillside every morning," he said, "that I may take off my cap each day to the wonder of God's world." When Jesus spoke his parables he very often founded them on the processes of nature. He saw God's power in the silently growing green things; he saw God's bounty in the harvest; he saw God's beauty in the scarlet anemones on the hillsides of Palestine.

Sir Christopher Wren is buried in St Paul's Cathedral of which he was the architect. On his stone there is a Latin sentence which means 'If you wish to see his monument, look around you.' If we wish to see God we must look around at the wonder of the world of which he is the architect.

A prayer: *O God, help me ever to see your beauty and your wonder in all common things.*

THE HEAVENS AND THE EARTH

Genesis 1:14-25

[14]And God said, "Let there be lights in the firmament of the heavens to separate the day from the night; and let them be for signs and for seasons and for days and years, [15]and let them be lights in the firmament of the heavens to give light upon the earth." And it was so. [16]And God made the two great lights, the greater light to rule the day, and the lesser light to rule the night; he made the stars also. ...

[20]And God said, "Let the waters bring forth swarms of living creatures, and let birds fly above the earth across the firmament of the heavens." [21]So God created the great sea monsters and every living creature that moves, with which the waters swarm, according to their kinds, and every winged bird according to its kind. And God saw that it was good. ...

[24]And God said, "Let the earth bring forth living creatures according to their kinds: cattle and creeping things and beasts of the earth according to their kinds." And it was so. [25]And God made the beasts of the earth according to their kinds and the cattle according to their kinds, and everything that creeps upon the ground according to its kind. And God saw that it was good.

From this passage we learn a great and comforting truth; God's power extends over the greatest things. The sun, moon and stars and the infinities of space are in his hands. The scientists tell us that an ordinary express train would take three hundred years to reach the sun; it would take seventy-five million years to reach the nearest fixed star: and it would take seven hundred million years to reach the Pole Star. Yet all these infinite, almost unthinkable spaces are in the hands of God. The farthest corner of the universe is not beyond his domain.

But also, God's power extends over the smallest things. Where there is life even in the smallest organism, there is God. God is the God of great things; yet he is also the God to whom the littlest detail of his universe is a precious thing.

To remember: *nothing and no one is either too great or too unimportant for God.*

IN THE IMAGE OF GOD

Genesis 1:26-8

[26]Then God said, "Let us make man in our image, after our likeness; and let them have dominion over the fish of the sea, and over the birds of the air, and over the cattle, and over all the earth, and over every creeping thing that creeps upon the earth." [27]So God created man in his own image, in the image of God he created him; male and female he created them. [28]And God blessed them, and God said to them, "Be fruitful and multiply, and fill the earth and subdue it; and have dominion over the fish of the sea and over the birds of the air and over every living thing that moves upon the earth."

Of all created things man has a special and unique kinship with God. The ancient Stoics believed that the soul of man was a spark of God which had come to live in a human body and that when man died that spark returned to God. The Greek called man *anthrōpos*, which means 'the upward looker'. Man by his very constitution and creation is created to look up. That is why as the moon moves the sea the thought of God moves the hearts of men. That is why man can never find fulness of life or unalloyed happiness or undisturbed peace apart from God. As Augustine said, "You have made us for yourself and our hearts are restless until they rest in you." But it is true that man can deface the image of God and it is to recreate us for that which we were first created that Jesus came and did his work.

A prayer: *O God, when I am tempted to lower and to lesser things make me to remember that you created me in your own image, and so keep me true to you.*

BEHOLD, IT WAS VERY GOOD

Genesis 1:29-31

> [29]And God said, "Behold, I have given you every plant yielding seed which is upon the face of all the earth, and every tree with seed in its fruit; you shall have them for food. [30]And to every beast of the earth, and to every bird of the air, and to everything that creeps on the earth, everything that has the breath of life, I have given every green plant for food." And it was so. [31]And God saw everything that he had made, and behold, it was very good.

In the primal springtime of the creation all things were very good. But man has sullied the fair creation of God. His selfishness has created the slums of the cities and the drabness of the industrial towns in his desire to get wealth, irrespective of how his fellow-men have to live. Man's hatred has scarred the face of earth with the wounds of war and the legacy of strife. Man's pride has sought to mould things to his plans instead of submitting to the plans of God.

When we think of the evil and ugliness of the world we must never resentfully blame God, rather let us kneel in humble penitence for the blots that men have made in God's fair creation.

For self-examination: *what am I doing to bring the beauty of God to my little corner of his creation?*

THE REST OF GOD

Genesis 2:1-3

[1]Thus the heavens and the earth were finished, and all the host of them. [2]And on the seventh day God finished his work which he had done, and he rested on the seventh day from all his work which he had done. [3]So God blessed the seventh day and hallowed it, because on it God rested from all his work which he had done in creation.

The Jews thought of the seventh day of the week, the Sabbath, as the day on which God rested from the work of creation and therefore as the day set apart for all time as the day of rest. The Christian Sunday is not the Jewish Sabbath. The Jewish Sabbath was Saturday, the last day of the week. The Christian Sunday is the first day of the week and commemorates the rising of Christ from the dead. But it remains a day of rest. In that it is essential.

During the French Revolution, Sunday was made an ordinary day. It had to be brought back again because the health of the nation was suffering from the lack of a day of rest. God gave us a time to labour and a time to rest. We must see to it that we ourselves observe the rest of God, and that we never demand pleasures which would make it necessary for others to work on the day of rest.

To pray: *O God, teach me to use your day to find rest from my body and strength for my soul.*

THE BREATH OF LIFE

Genesis 2:4-7

[4]These are the generations of the heavens and the earth when they were created.

In the day that the LORD God made the earth and the heavens, [5]when no plant of the field was yet in the earth and no herb of the field had yet sprung up — for the LORD God had not caused it to rain upon the earth, and there was no man to till the ground; [6]but a mist went up from the earth and watered the whole face of the ground — [7]then the LORD God formed man of dust from the ground, and breathed into his nostrils the breath of life; and man became a living being.

The great symbolic truth enshrined here is the truth that the life that man possesses is the life of God. Man in his skill and cleverness has achieved many things; but man has never succeeded in creating life. We can make this and that and the next synthetic substitute; but man has never succeeded in making life.* A scientist can analyse a seed into its constituent elements. He can make a synthetic seed of just these elements. It will look like a real seed and it will have in it all the chemical elements which are in a real seed: but *it will not grow*. It is God and God only who can breathe life into man and all his creation. We therefore are bound to come to the essential and the fundamental conclusion of life — that the life we have is not our own, for it was both created and redeemed by God.

A prayer: *you have made me, O God, and I am yours: you have redeemed me and I am doubly yours. Help me to give back to you the life I owe.*

*This was written in 1950, of course, since when science has advanced enormously, not least in understanding and manipulating DNA.

THE GARDEN AND THE TREE

Genesis 2:8-17

[8]And the LORD God planted a garden in Eden, in the east; and there he put the man whom he had formed. [9]And out of the ground the LORD God made to grow every tree that is pleasant to the sight and good for food, the tree of life also in the midst of the garden, and the tree of the knowledge of good and evil. ...

[15]The LORD God took the man and put him in the garden of Eden to till it and keep it. [16]And the LORD God commanded the man, saying, ''You may freely eat of every tree of the garden; [17]but of the tree of the knowledge of good and evil you shall not eat, for in the day that you eat of it you shall die.''

Even in the garden of the paradise of Eden there are things which a man must not do. Man was created for obedience. We must learn that here and there in life there are signposts and warnings which say to us, 'This far and no farther'. There is that in us which tells us when to stop, the voice we call the voice of conscience.

The penalty of disobedience is always heavy. But we must ever remember that when we suffer for disobedience it is not God who has punished us so much as it is we who have brought punishment upon ourselves. The old Greeks had a thought which recurs in their highest thinkers again and again, like a text running through a sermon — 'The doer shall suffer.' They believed that it was woven into the warp and woof of the universe that sin always found its punishment.

There is only one way to happiness. We shall find life in submission to God and we shall find peace only in doing his will.

A prayer: *teach me, O God, to say in all things: your will be done.*

MAN MUST NOT BE ALONE

Genesis 2: 18-25

[18]Then the LORD God said, "It is not good that the man should be alone; I will make him a helper fit for him." [19]So out of the ground the LORD God formed every beast of the field and every bird of the air, and brought them to the man to see what he would call them; and whatever the man called every living creature, that was its name. [20]The man gave names to all cattle, and to the birds of the air, and to every beast of the field; but for the man there was not found a helper fit for him. [21]So the LORD God caused a deep sleep to fall upon the man, and while he slept took one of his ribs and closed up its place with flesh; [22]and the rib which the LORD God had taken from the man he made into a woman and brought her to the man. [23]Then the man said,

"This at last is bone of my bones
and flesh of my flesh;
she shall be called Woman,
because she was taken out of
Man."

[24]Therefore a man leaves his father and his mother and cleaves to his wife, and they become one flesh. [26]And the man and his wife were both naked and were not ashamed.

Man was created for fellowship. Life which is lived alone is not full life. He is created for the fellowship of his fellow-men. At an early period in his Christian life John Wesley proposed to retire into the wilds and to build himself a cabin there and live in lonely prayer and contemplation. An older and wiser Christian said to him, 'God knows nothing of solitary religion.' We find life not in hoarding it in lonely isolation but in pouring it out in fellowship.

Man is created for the fellowship of God. Over and over again the psychologists will tell a man that the cause of the breakdown of his mind is that he has failed to find contact with a power beyond himself. Without the friendship of men we are lonely; without the friendship of God we are incomplete.

A thought: *I must remember that 'a man should keep his friendships in constant repair.'*

THE ATTACK OF TEMPTATION

Genesis 3:1-7

> [1]Now the serpent was more subtle than any other wild creature that the LORD God had made. He said to the woman, "Did God say, 'You shall not eat of any tree of the garden'?" [2]And the woman said to the serpent, "We may eat of the fruit of the trees of the garden; [3]but God said, 'You shall not eat of the fruit of the tree which is in the midst of the garden, neither shall you touch it, lest you die.' " [4]But the serpent said to the woman, "You will not die. [5]For God knows that when you eat of it your eyes will be opened, and you will be like God, knowing good and evil." [6]So when the woman saw that the tree was good for food, and that it was a delight to the eyes, and that the tree was to be desired to make one wise, she took of its fruit and ate; and she also gave some to her husband, and he ate. [7]Then the eyes of both were opened, and they knew that they were naked; and they sewed fig leaves together and made themselves aprons.

This story tells not so much of a thing which happened once in the dim and distant past, but of something which is happening to every man every day in life.

Verse 6 tells us of the method and the attack of temptation. (i) The forbidden thing looked as if it was good for food. The forbidden thing always looks as if it would bring us happiness. (ii) It was pleasant to the eyes. The forbidden thing always has a certain meretricious attraction about it. (iii) It looked as if it was to be desired to make one wise. The forbidden thing always promises to confer benefits upon us. We think life would be much happier and much better if only we had it.

It is just in these things that the subtlety of temptation lies. If the forbidden thing was ugly, repulsive and completely undesirable no one would ever fall to temptation. But the tempter dresses things up in such a way that they look attractive and look as if they would bring happiness. The only way to avoid temptation is to love the supreme beauty of Jesus Christ and his goodness so much that no lesser thing will ever attract us.

A prayer: *O God, help me to see things as they really are and not to be led away by things which look good but which lead to death.*

THE SINNER'S EXCUSE

Genesis 3:8-13

[8]And they heard the sound of the LORD God walking in the garden in the cool of the day, and the man and his wife hid themselves from the presence of the LORD God among the trees of the garden. [9]But the LORD God called to the man, and said to him, "Where are you?" [10]And he said, "I heard the sound of thee in the garden, and I was afraid, because I was naked; and I hid myself." [11]He said, "Who told you that you were naked? Have you eaten of the tree of which I commanded you not to eat?" [12]The man said, "The woman whom thou gavest to be with me, she gave me the fruit of the tree, and I ate." [13]Then the LORD God said to the woman, "What is this that you have done?" The woman said, "The serpent beguiled me, and I ate."

Here again we have something which is happening every day. Read again verses 12 and 13. See how first Adam and then Eve try to shuffle out of their responsibility and to put the blame on someone else. Adam says, don't blame me; blame the woman. Eve says, don't blame me: blame the serpent. When we have done something wrong our first instinct is to make excuses and to try to put the blame on persons or on circumstances outside ourselves.

When we sin there is only one way to forgiveness and peace. We too must say, 'I will arise and go to my Father and I will say to him, Father, I have sinned.' The way to forgiveness lies not through excuses, but through the contrite heart.

For self-examination: *when things go wrong, do I blame everything and everyone except myself?*

12

THE HARDNESS OF LIFE

Genesis 3:16-20

¹⁶To the woman he said,

"I will greatly multiply your pain in
childbearing;
in pain you shall bring forth
children,
yet your desire shall be for your
husband,
and he shall rule over you."

¹⁷And to Adam he said,

"Because you have listened to the
voice of your wife,
and have eaten of the tree
of which I commanded you,
'You shall not eat of it,'
cursed is the ground because of you;
in toil you shall eat of it all the
days of your life;
¹⁸thorns and thistles it shall bring
forth to you;
and you shall eat the plants of
the field.
¹⁹In the sweat of your face
you shall eat bread
till you return to the ground,
for out of it you were taken;
you are dust,
and to dust you shall return."

²⁰The man called his wife's name Eve, because she was the mother of all living.

The truth at the heart of this old story is that when sin enters life, it becomes a grim and unhappy thing.

Sin casts a shadow upon life. (i) It casts a shadow on our relationship with ourselves. A man has always got to live with himself, and he cannot be happy unless he can meet his own eyes and respect himself. (ii)It casts a shadow on our relationship with others. When we have wronged someone, even if that person is unaware of it, there is a barrier between us and that person all the time. (iii) It casts a barrier between us and God. *Genesis* 3:8 tells us that the first thing Adam and Eve did was to try to hide themselves. The sinner who realises what he has done always attempts the impossible task of hiding from God.

A prayer: *save me, O God, from doing anything that would come between me and my fellow-men or that would come between me and you.*

MY BROTHER'S KEEPER

Genesis 4:3-9

[3]In the course of time Cain brought to the LORD an offering of the fruit of the ground, [4]and Abel brought of the firstlings of his flock and of their fat portions. And the LORD had regard for Abel and his offering, [5]but for Cain and his offering he had no regard. So Cain was very angry, and his countenance fell. [6]The LORD said to Cain, ''Why are you angry, and why has your countenance fallen? [7]If you do well, will you not be accepted? And if you do not do well, sin is couching at the door; its desire is for you, but you must master it.''

[8]Cain said to Abel his brother, ''Let us go out to the field.'' And when they were in the field, Cain rose up against his brother Abel, and killed him. [9]Then the LORD said to Cain, ''Where is Abel your brother?'' He said, ''I do not know; am I my brother's keeper?''

Cain's defiant defence for his sin is to demand from God, 'Am I my brother's keeper?' and God's answer is 'You are.' In this life we are all bound up together in the bundle of life. No man lives to himself and no man dies to himself. We are responsible not only for what we do with our own lives but for the impact that we have on the lives of others. We must learn to pray and to live St Francis's prayer:

Lord, make me an instrument of your peace. Where there is hatred, let me sow love. Where there is injury, pardon. Where there is doubt, faith. Where there is despair, hope. Where there is darkness, light. Where there is sorrow, joy. O Divine Master, grant that I may not so much seek to be consoled, as to console; to be understood, as to understand; to be loved, as to love; for it is in giving that we receive, it is in pardoning that we are pardoned, and it is in dying that we are born to eternal life.

A question: *read St Francis' prayer again. Now ask, how nearly does my life approach to that?*

THE ONE MAN WHO FOUND GRACE

Genesis 6:1-3,5-8

[1]When men began to multiply on the face of the ground, and daughters were born to them, [2]the sons of God saw that the daughters of men were fair; and they took to wife such of them as they chose. [3]Then the LORD said, ''My spirit shall not abide in man for ever, for he is flesh, but his days shall be a hundred and twenty years.'' ...

[5]The LORD saw that the wickedness of man was great in the earth, and that every imagination of the thoughts of his heart was only evil continually. [6]And the LORD was sorry that he had made man on the earth, and it grieved him to his heart. [7]So the LORD said, ''I will blot out man whom I have created from the face of the ground, man and beast and creeping things and birds of the air, for I am sorry that I have made them.'' [8]But Noah found favour in the eyes of the LORD.

There is a tragic picture here. There is the picture of degeneration. Sin entered into the world. Man went his own proud way. There seemed to be left for God no cure for things but the obliteration of mankind.

There is an uplifting picture here. For amid this there was one man who still kept faith with God. Noah is the supreme example of a man who rose above his environment: a man who kept his garments unspotted in an evil world. We cannot blame society for our sins. The man whose heart is fixed to God has an inner antiseptic which defends him against the poisons of the world.

For meditation: *am I content to be like the world? Or do I try to be different from the world?*

THE DEPENDABILITY OF GOD

Genesis 8:20-22

[20]Then Noah built an altar to the LORD, and took of every clean animal and of every clean bird, and offered burnt offerings on the altar. [21]And when the LORD smelled the pleasing odour, the LORD said in his heart, ''I will never again curse the ground because of man, for the imagination of man's heart is evil from his youth; neither will I ever again destroy every living creature as I have done. [22]While the earth remains, seedtime and harvest, cold and heat, summer and winter, day and night, shall not cease.''

Read again verse 22. Does it never strike us to give God thanks that we live in so dependable a world? What would life be like if when darkness fell we did not know whether or not the morning would come again? What would life be like if when winter came we did not know if spring would ever again bring new life? What would life be like if when we sowed the seed we did not know whether the harvest would ever follow? There are things which come to us so regularly and so unfailingly that often we forget that they are God's gifts to us.

Let us remember that the faithfulness of God is reflected in the unfailing order of his universe.

A thought: *let us give God thanks for the unfailing power and love behind the order of the universe.*

LIFE BELONGS TO GOD

Genesis 9:1-6

[1]And God blessed Noah and his sons, and said to them, "Be fruitful and multiply, and fill the earth. [2]The fear of you and the dread of you shall be upon every beast of the earth, and upon every bird of the air, upon everything that creeps on the ground and all the fish of the sea; into your hand they are delivered. [3]Every moving thing that lives shall be food for you; and as I gave you the green plants, I give you everything. [4]Only you shall not eat flesh with its life, that is, its blood. [5]For your lifeblood I will surely require a reckoning; of every beast I will require it and of man; of every man's brother I will require the life of man. [6]Whoever sheds the blood of man, by man shall his blood be shed; for God made man in his own image.

The Jew identified blood with life. If a man was wounded, his blood ebbed out and with the blood his life ebbed away. Very naturally the Jew came to the conclusion that the blood was the life. Therefore the Jew would never eat anything out of which the blood had not been drained away and offered to God. We see that even in New Testament times. Acts 15:20 tells how the Council of Jerusalem laid it down that the Gentiles must abstain from blood. To this day Jewish law decrees that animals must be killed in such a way that the blood will drain off before the meat is eaten, because the blood belongs to God.

Behind all that there lies the great truth that all life belongs to God; all life is God's. To take any man's life is to take that which belongs to God. Our duty is to use our own life nobly, and to make it possible for others to use theirs nobly because life is of God.

A prayer: *O God, help me to remember that my life is yours: help me to remember that my neighbour's life is yours: and help me so to live that I may use life greatly, and help others to use it greatly, and that I may never destroy it.*

THE BOW IN THE CLOUDS

Genesis 9:8-16

[8]Then God said to Noah, and to his sons with him, [9]"Behold, I establish my covenant with you and your descendants after you, [10]and with every living ceature that is with you, the birds, the cattle, and every beast of the earth with you, as many as came out of the ark. [11]I establish my covenant with you, that never again shall all flesh be cut off by the waters of a flood, and never again shall there be a flood to destroy the earth". [12]And God said, "This is the sign of the covenant which I make between me and you and every living creature that is with you, for all future generations: [13]I set my bow in the cloud, and it shall be a sign of the covenant between me and the earth. [14]When I bring clouds over the earth and the bow is seen in the clouds, [15]I will remember my covenant which is between me and you and every living creature of all flesh; and the waters shall never again become a flood to destroy all flesh. [16]When the bow is in the clouds, I will look upon it and remember the everlasting covenant between God and every living creature of all flesh that is upon the earth."

Ancient peoples were very like children. They loved to tell stories which explained the things that happened in nature. So they looked at the many-coloured wonder of the rainbow and felt that it was none other than a sign of the promise of God that his all-consuming wrath would not go out upon his people again.

We live in a world which is full of God. The world is 'the garment of the living God'. The sight of the sun, the moon, the stars, the hillside, the sea, all green things and all living creatures, should turn our minds to the God who is in it and behind it all and by whom all nature lives and the world stands. It is a lovely thing to live in a world where the rainbow speaks to us of God.

A prayer: *open my eyes, O God, that I may see you in the world your hands have made and your love upholds.*

THE PRIDE OF MAN

Genesis 11:1-9

[1]Now the whole earth had one language and few words. [2]And as men migrated from the east, they found a plain in the land of Shinar and settled there. [3]And they said to one another, "Come, let us make bricks, and burn them thoroughly." And they had brick for stone, and bitumen for mortar. [4]Then they said, "Come, let us build ourselves a city, and a tower with its top in the heavens, and let us make a name for ourselves, lest we be scattered abroad upon the face of the whole earth." [5]And the LORD came down to see the city and the tower, which the sons of men had built. [6]And the LORD said, "Behold, they are one people, and they have all one language; and this is only the beginning of what they will do; and nothing that they propose to do will now be impossible for them. [7]Come, let us go down, and there confuse their language, that they may not understand one another's speech." [8]So the LORD scattered them abroad from there over the face of all the earth, and they left off building the city. [9]Therefore its name was called Babel, because there the LORD confused the language of all the earth; and from there the LORD scattered them abroad over the face of all the earth.

At the heart of this old story is the eternal truth that pride and overweening ambition set men at enmity with each other, and at enmity with God. If there is overreaching pride at the heart of a man, it makes every man his enemy. For then it becomes his aim to overreach his fellow-men and to exalt himself above them. Anyone who gets in his way and hinders him has to be crushed and eliminated. That pride can operate in little things just as well as in great.

Further, pride alienates a man from God. A man can only come to God on his knees. Religion starts with an act of humble submission to God. The pride that will not stoop has shut itself off from God.

For self-examination: *if I find within myself any remnants of pride, let me tear them from my heart.*

AN ADVENTURER FOR GOD

Genesis 12:1-5

> [1]Now the LORD said to Abram, ''Go from your country and your kindred and your father's house to the land that I will show you. [2]And I will make of you a great nation, and I will bless you, and make your name great, so that you will be a blessing. [3]I will bless those who bless you, and him who curses you I will curse; and by you all the families of the earth shall bless themselves.''
>
> [4]So Abram went as the LORD had told him; and Lot went with him. Abram was seventy-five years old when he departed from Haran. [5]And Abram took Sar'ai his wife, and Lot his brother's son, and all their possessions which they had gathered, and the persons that they had gotten in Haran; and they set forth to go to the land of Canaan. When they had come to the land of Canaan. ...

Somehow God revealed himself to Abraham. Abraham knew that in the environment and society in which he lived he could not worship God as he knew he must worship him. So, as the writer to the Hebrews has it (11:8), he went out, 'not knowing where he was to go'.

There are two great thoughts here. (i) To live the Christian life is to make a clean break with the past. When a man becomes a pledged follower of Christ, it is as if a line were drawn in his life after which everything is different. That is a hard beginning to make. (ii) To live the Christian life is to be certain of the happy ending. Verse 5 ends greatly: 'They set forth to go to the land of Canaan. When they had come to the land of Canaan. ...' It tells us nothing of the long journey, of the hardships and the difficulties and the weariness of the way. Why? Because in the joy of the goal the hardness of the journey was forgotten.

At the end of the day a man who has followed Christ will forget all else in the joy of being with his Lord.

A prayer: *O God, grant that I may think not of the hardness of the way, but of the glory of the goal.*

NO THOUGHT OF SELF

Genesis 13:1-9

[1]So Abram went up from Egypt, he and his wife, and all that he had, and Lot with him, into the Negeb.

[2]Now Abram was very rich in cattle, in silver, and in gold. [3]And he journeyed on from the Negeb as far as Bethel, to the place where his tent had been at the beginning, between Bethel and Ai, [4]to the place where he had made an altar at the first; and there Abram called on the name of the LORD. [5]And Lot, who went with Abram, also had flocks and herds and tents, [6]so that the land could not support both of them dwelling together; for their possessions were so great that they could not dwell together, [7]and there was strife between the herdsmen of Abram's cattle and the herdsmen of Lot's cattle. ...

[8]Then Abram said to Lot, "Let there be no strife between you and me, and between your herdsmen and my herdsmen. [9]Is not the whole land before you? Separate yourself from me. If you take the left hand, then I will go to the right; or if you take the right hand, then I will go to the left."

Great sheep and cattle masters like Abraham and Lot needed much pasture and many wells to support their flocks. The land was not enough to support both. So Abraham offered Lot his choice of direction. Lot chose the good and fertile land, leaving to Abraham the rough highland country; but Abraham made no complaint.

The mark of the man of God is the unselfish spirit. He remembers that he who will be greatest must be the servant of all. The world thinks in terms of self-assertion; Christ thinks in terms of self-sacrifice. History proves that Christ was right because it is not the great conquerors but the great servants whom humanity remembers with honour.

To think about: *am I ever guilty of self-assertion? Do I really act as if I believed that he who would be greatest in the kingdom of heaven must be the servant of all?*

THE COVENANT OF GOD

Genesis 17:1-5,9-10

[1]When Abram was ninety-nine years old the LORD appeared to Abram, and said to him, "I am God Almighty; walk before me, and be blameless. [2]And I will make my covenant between me and you, and will multiply you exceedingly." [3]Then Abram fell on his face; and God said to him, [4] "Behold, my covenant is with you, and you shall be the father of a multitude of nations. [5]No longer shall your name be Abram, but your name shall be Abraham; for I have made you the father of a multitude of nations. ...

[9]And God said to Abraham, "As for you, you shall keep my covenant, you and your descendants after you throughout their generations. [10]This is my covenant, which you shall keep, between me and you and your descendants after you: Every male among you shall be circumcised.

Over and over again the bible speaks of a covenant relationship. In a covenant God approaches the nation that they may be his people; and the nation in answer pledges itself to live for ever according to the laws and commands of God.

This passage tells how God made his covenant with Abraham and how Abraham pledged himself to God. All Abraham's male descendants were to bear upon their bodies the visible mark of that covenant. But as men began to know more and more about God they began to see that it was not a mark upon the body but a mark upon the heart and soul which stamped a man as God's man.

The question is not, have I some physical mark which shows me to be God's man? The question is, have I the heart, the mind, the character which proves that I am God's?

A prayer: *O God, help me to be so fine, so pure, so true that others shall see your mark upon me and know that I am yours.*

THE PATIENCE OF GOD

Genesis 18:23-33

[23]Then Abraham drew near, and said, "Wilt thou indeed destroy the righteous with the wicked? [24]Suppose there are fifty righteous within the city; wilt thou then destroy the place and not spare it for the fifty righteous who are in it? [25]Far be it from thee to do such a thing, to slay the righteous with the wicked, so that the righteous fare as the wicked! Far be that from thee! Shall not the Judge of all the earth do right?" [26]And the LORD said, "If I find at Sodom fifty righteous in the city, I will spare the whole place for their sake." [27]Abraham answered, "Behold, I have taken upon myself to speak to the Lord, I who am but dust and ashes. [28]Suppose five of the fifty righteous are lacking? Wilt thou destroy the whole city for lack of five?" And he said, "I will not destroy it if I find forty-five there." [29]Again he spoke to him, and said, "Suppose forty are found there." He answered, "For the sake of forty I will not do it." [30]Then he said, "Oh let not the LORD be angry, and I will speak. Suppose thirty are found there." He answered, "I will not do it, if I find thirty there." [31]He said, "Behold, I have taken upon myself to speak to the LORD. Suppose twenty are found there." He answered, "For the sake of twenty I will not destroy it." [32]Then he said, "Oh let not the LORD be angry, and I will speak again but this once. Suppose ten are found there." He answered, "For the sake of ten I will not destroy it." [33]And the LORD went his way, when he had finished speaking to Abraham; and Abraham returned to his place.

The cities of the plain were very wicked and God forewarned Abraham of their destruction. This old story tells us three things.

(i)   The good man is merciful. Abraham was a good man and yet in spite of his goodness he did not yearn for the destruction of sinners. He was not hard and intolerant; he wished to see the cities spared and not destroyed.

(ii)   It tells us that the last thing God wishes is to wipe men out. The patience of God is stretched to the limits; the mercy of God is spread to the utmost; God desires not the death of a sinner but rather that he should repent and live.

(iii)   But it also tells us that there is a limit. Evil cannot reign unchecked and vice cannot be unrestrainedly rampant. Sooner or later if God's appeals fall on deaf ears, God's judgment comes.

A prayer: *O Lord, give to me that spirit which loves mercy and yet will not compromise with sin.*

THE BACKWARD LOOK

Genesis 19:15-26

[15]When morning dawned, the angels urged Lot, saying, "Arise, take your wife and your two daughters who are here, lest you be consumed in the punishment of the city." [16]But he lingered; so the men seized him and his wife and his two daughters by the hand, the LORD being merciful to him, and they brought him forth and set him outside the city. [17]And when they had brought them forth, they said, "Flee for your life; do not look back or stop anywhere in the valley; flee to the hills, lest you be consumed." [18]And Lot said to them, "Oh, no, my lords; [19]behold, your servant has found favour in your sight, and you have shown me great kindness in saving my life; but I cannot flee to the hills, lest the disaster overtake me, and I die. [20]Behold, yonder city is near enought to flee to, and it is a little one. Let me escape there — is it not a little one? — and my life will be saved!" [21]He said to him, "Behold, I grant you this favour also, that I will not overthrow the city of which you have spoken. [22]Make haste, escape there; for I can do nothing till you arrive there." Therefore the name of the city was called Zo'ar. [23]The sun had risen on the earth when Lot came to Zo'ar.

[24]Then the LORD rained on Sodom and Gomor'rah brimstone and fire from the LORD out of heaven; [25]and he overthrew those cities, and all the valley, and all the inhabitants of the cities, and what grew on the ground. [26]But Lot's wife behind him looked back, and she became a pillar of salt.

Lot's wife has become a proverb. When we make a decision it should be a definite decision. There should be no longing, lingering backward looks. If a man keeps looking backward at that which he has left it means that it has still some place within and hold upon his heart. It means that the last idol is not torn out. Jesus said, 'No man having put his hand to the plough, and looking back, is fit for the kingdom of God' (*Luke* 9:62).

This does not mean that we must never fall, but that however often we fall our eyes must still be upon the distant goal. We must be as those who 'never turn their backs but march breast forward'. Christ should be the *only* Lord of our hearts.

For self-examination: *do I ever court danger by letting my looks linger on things which I ought to leave behind me for good?*

ALL FOR GOD

Genesis 22:1-3,9-11

¹After these things God tested Abraham, and said to him, "Abraham!" And he said, "Here am I." ²He said, "Take your son, your only son Isaac, whom you love, and go to the land of Moriah, and offer him there as a burnt offering upon one of the mountains of which I shall tell you." ³So Abraham rose early in the morning, saddled his ass, and took two of his young men with him, and his son Isaac; and he cut the wood for the burnt offering, and arose and went to the place of which God had told him.
...

⁹When they came to the place of which God had told him, Abraham built an altar there, and laid the wood in order, and bound Isaac his son, and laid him on the altar, upon the wood. ¹⁰Then Abraham put forth his hand, and took the knife to slay his son. ¹¹But the angel of the LORD called to him from heaven, and said, "Abraham!" And he said, "Here am I."

We know now that God would never ask a man to sacrifice his son. But we also know that Jesus said, 'He that loves father or mother more than me is not worthy of me: and he that loves son or daughter more than me is not worthy of me' (*Matthew* 10:37). The claim of God must take precedence over all other claims.

In the early church it must often have been the case that a man had to choose between his family ties and Christ. What Abraham did on this occasion was to pass the supreme test of loyalty and to demonstrate that no matter what God asked of him he would do it.

> The dearest idol I have known,
>> Whate'er that idol be,
> Help me to tear it from Thy throne,
>> And worship only Thee.

For quiet meditation: *read that verse again. Can I honestly pray that prayer? Or are there things that I have no intention of giving up?*

NO GOING BACK

Genesis 24:1-6

¹Now Abraham was old, well advanced in years; and the LORD had blessed Abraham in all things. ²And Abraham said to his servant, the oldest of his house, who had charge of all that he had, "Put your hand under my thigh, ³and I will make you swear by the LORD, the God of heaven and of the earth, that you will not take a wife for my son from the daughters of the Canaanites, among whom I dwell, ⁴but will go to my country and to my kindred, and take a wife for my son Isaac." ⁵The servant said to him, "Perhaps the woman may not be willing to follow me to this land; must I then take your son back to the land from which you came?" ⁶Abraham said to him, "See to it that you do not take my son back there. ..."

In this story of how Abraham sought to find a wife for his son Isaac there is all the wisdom of a man who had seen and lived life and learned its lesson.

(i) He wanted for Isaac a wife of his own kindred, his own blood and his own people. It is one of the basic facts of human relationships that true friendships and true love can never be between those whose traditions are entirely different. Passion is a moment's flame, but love is a light that must burn down all the years. To live together people must share a common heritage and a common tradition.

(ii) But for all that, Abraham did not want his son Isaac to go back to the country from which he himself had come. Abraham knew that one of the surest ways to avoid temptation is never to flirt with danger. He did not want his son to be exposed to any evil influence. He was determined that he who had started on the new way must not go back to the old.

THE TEST OF KINDNESS

Genesis 24:10-14

[10]Then the servant took ten of his master's camels and departed, taking all sorts of choice gifts from his master; and he arose, and went to Mesopota'mia, to the city of Nahor. [11]And he made the camels kneel down outside the city by the well of water at the time of evening, the time when women go out to draw water. [12]And he said, "O LORD, God of my master Abraham, grant me success today, I pray thee, and show steadfast love to my master Abraham [13]Behold, I am standing by the spring of water, and the daughters of the men of the city are coming out to draw water. [14]Let the maiden to whom I shall say, 'Pray let down your jar that I may drink,' and who shall say, 'Drink, and I will water your camels' — let her be the one whom thou hast appointed for thy servant Isaac. By this I shall know that thou hast shown steadfast love to my master."

The servant's test was very simple. He would seek to bring home the maiden who not only gave him to drink at the well but gave his camels to drink also.

His test was the test of kindness. What he wanted was a young woman whose heart was such that she could neither bear to see the wayfaring man nor the wayfaring beast thirsty and tired. There are qualities and brilliancies which dazzle, and fade. True friendship and love can only be founded on the qualities which wear well: and there is none which is such a sure foundation for future happiness as the heart that is kind.

A question for today: *do I seek to dazzle men? Or do I seek to help them?*

USE HOSPITALITY TO ALL MEN

Genesis 24: 15-21

[15]Before he had done speaking, behold, Rebekah, who was born to Bethu'el the son of Milcah, the wife of Nahor, Abraham's brother, came out with her water jar upon her shoulder. [16]The maiden was very fair to look upon, a virgin, whom no man had known. She went down to the spring, and filled her jar, and came up. [17]Then the servant ran to meet her, and said, "Pray give me a little water to drink from your jar." [18]She said, "Drink, my lord"; and she quickly let down her jar upon her hand, and gave him a drink. [19]When she had finished giving him a drink, she said, "I will draw for your camels also, until they have done drinking." [20]So she quickly emptied her jar into the trough and ran again to the well to draw, and she drew for all his camels. [21] The man gazed at her in silence to learn whether the LORD had prospered his journey or not.

See with what hospitality Rebekah welcomes the wayfarer.

It is curious how the bible lays stress on the simple virtue of the hospitable heart. When he writes to the Romans, Paul insists that the follower of Christ should be given hospitality (*Romans* 12:13). The first letter to Timothy insists that the leader of the Church must be given to hospitality (I *Timothy* 3:2). The letter to Titus declares that the Christian minister must be a lover of hospitality (*Titus* 1:8). The first letter of Peter bids Christian folk, 'Use hospitality to one another without grudging' (I *Peter* 4:9).

A great tribute paid to one of the old Greeks was, 'He lived in a house by the side of the road and he was a friend of wayfaring men.' We did not get our homes selfishly to shut the door, but that they might be centres of fellowship in Christ.

A prayer: *O God, help me to love you as you have loved me, and then help me to love my fellow-men as you love them.*

IT IS GOD'S WILL

Genesis 24:34-41,50

[34]So he said, "I am Abraham's servant. [35]The LORD has greatly blessed my master, and he has become great; he has given him flocks and herds, silver and gold, menservants and maidservants, camels and asses. [36]And Sarah my master's wife bore a son to my master when he was old; and to him he has given all that he has. [37] My master made me swear, saying, 'You shall not take a wife for my son from the daughters of the Canaanites, in whose land I dwell; [38]but you shall go to my father's house and to my kindred, and take a wife for my son.' [39]I said to my master, 'Perhaps the woman will not follow me.' [40]But he said to me, "The LORD, before whom I walk, will send his angel with you and prosper your way, and you shall take a wife for my son from my kindred and from my father's house; [41]then you will be free from my oath, when you come to my kindred; and if they will not give her to you, you will be free from my oath.' ...

[50]Then Laban and Bethu'el answered, "The thing comes from the LORD; we cannot speak to you bad or good. ..."

Read verse 50 again. Blessed is the man who sees God's hand in the events of everyday life. Sometimes people say they do not know where their duty lies and they do not know what they ought to do. God gave us the voice of conscience speaking within our hearts. He gave to us the promptings of his Holy Spirit. The times when a man is in any real doubt as to what he ought to do are far fewer than sometimes we would wish to believe. So often our doubts regarding any suggested course of action are not real doubts, but simply the outcome of the struggle between our wills and what we know in our heart of hearts is the will of God.

There *is* a guiding hand in life. When we stand at the crossroads of life there is a guiding light and sure signpost. God give us the humility to accept the guidance which always comes to us and not to fight against it.

A resolution to make: *I will resolve in every course of action to listen to God's voice, and to obey it.*

THE LOVELY VIRTUES

Genesis 24:58-67

⁵⁸And they called Rebekah, and said to her, "Will you go with this man?" She said, "I will go." ⁵⁹So they sent away Rebekah their sister and her nurse, and Abraham's servant and his men. ⁶⁰And they blessed Rebekah, and said to her, "Our sister, be the mother of thousands of ten thousands; and may your descendants possess the gate of those who hate them!" ⁶¹Then Rebekah and her maids arose, and rode upon the camels and followed the man; thus the servant took Rebekah, and went his way.

⁶²Now Isaac had come from Beer-la'hai-roi, and was dwelling in the Negeb. ⁶³And Isaac went out to meditate in the field in the evening; and he lifted up his eyes and looked, and behold, there were camels coming. ⁶⁴And Rebekah lifted up her eyes, and when she saw Isaac, she alighted from the camel, ⁶⁵and said to the servant, "Who is the man yonder, walking in the field to meet us?" The servant said, "It is my master." So she took her veil and covered herself. ⁶⁶And the servant told Isaac all the things that he had done. ⁶⁷Then Isaac brought her into the tent, and took Rebekah, and she became his wife, and he loved her. So Isaac was comforted after his mother's death.

The more we dwell upon this lovely chapter the more we see the fragrance of Rebekah's character. Verse 58 speaks of her humility. When the way is clear before her she seeks no delay, but, without question, she will go where the guiding hand of God will take her.

Verses 64 and 65 speak of her modesty. She comes without any flamboyant display. She alights from her camel and veils her face that she may enter quietly and modestly into the new life which lies before her.

Verse 67 tells of the comfort she brought to Isaac. Of all the gifts that anyone can bring to another human being the greatest is comfort. Sir William Watson said that the greatest of Wordsworth's qualities was that 'he had for weary feet the gift of rest.' So many people are restless and unquiet. So many bring into life an element of disturbance and unease. The most valuable people in the world are the people to whom we can go when we are tired, and when life has hurt us, in whose presence is peace. They bear upon themselves the reflection of the Master whose greeting was 'Peace be with you.'

A thought for today: *may I bring peace wherever I go.*

THE SHORT VIEW

Genesis 25:27-34

27When the boys grew up, Esau was a skilful hunter, a man of the field, while Jacob was a quiet man, dwelling in tents. 28Isaac loved Esau, because he ate of his game, but Rebekah loved Jacob.

29Once when Jacob was boiling pottage, Esau came in from the field, and he was famished. 30And Esau said to Jacob, "Let me eat some of that red pottage, for I am famished!" (Therefore his name was called Edom.) 31Jacob said, "First sell me your birthright." 32Esau said, "I am about to die; of what use is a birthright to me?" 33Jacob said, "Swear to me first."

So he swore to him, and sold his birthright to Jacob. 34Then Jacob gave Esau bread and pottage of lentils, and he ate and drank, and rose and went on his way. Thus Esau despised his birthright.

Esau is the eternal example of a man who took the short view of things. To gain a momentary pleasure in satisfying his hunger, he flung away his birthright.

There is nothing more necessary in life than to learn to take the long view. There are many things which seem pleasant for the moment but which in the long run can work nothing but harm. Many pleasures which seem desirable for the moment leave a bitter taste to follow. A man should be so master of himself that his impulses and passions are under control; that he may see things in the shadow of eternity instead of in the heat of the moment. There is many a thing we would not do and many a word we would not speak if we thought beyond the moment and looked ahead.

The Christian must look beyond time and into eternity, for in everything he does he is building a character which some day he will take with him to the presence and judgment of God.

A prayer: *O God, help me to see things as you see them, that I may ever put first things first.*

THE MIGHT OF MEEKNESS

Genesis 26:12-14,16-22

¹²And Isaac sowed in that land, and reaped in the same year a hundredfold. The LORD blessed him, ¹³and the man became rich, and gained more and more until he became very wealthy. ¹⁴ He had possessions of flocks and herds, and a great household, so that the Philistines envied him. ... ¹⁶And Abim'elech said to Isaac, "Go away from us; for you are much mightier than we."

¹⁷So Isaac departed from there, and encamped in the valley of Gerar and dwelt there. ¹⁸And Isaac dug again the wells of water which had been dug in the days of Abraham his father; for the Philistines had stopped them after the death of Abraham; and he gave them the names which his father had given them. ¹⁹But when Isaac's servants dug in the valley and found there a well of springing water, ²⁰ the herdsmen of Gerar quarrelled with Isaac's herdsmen, saying, "The water is ours." So he called the name of the well Esek, because they contended with him. ²¹Then they dug another well, and they quarrelled over that also; so he called its name Sitnah. ²²And he moved from there and dug another well, and over that they did not quarrel; so he called its name Reho'both, saying, "For now the LORD has made room for us, and we shall be fruitful in the land."

If we knew nothing of Isaac save what these few verses tell us, he would still be for ever a lovely character. He was pre-eminently the man who would not fight. This quality of gentleness has always been a characteristic of the Christian spirit. 'The servant of the Lord must not strive; but be gentle to all men' (2 *Timothy* 2:24). The Christian duty is to be 'no brawlers, but gentle, showing all meekness to all men' (*Titus* 3:2).

And it is true that the meek inherit the earth. A scimitar will cut even a bar of iron, but it cannot cut a feather pillow. A great railway, when crossing a marsh and a bog, had finally had to be laid upon faggots. Other things sunk in the mire; only the faggots would support it. Someone has spoken of 'the irresistible might of meekness.' The true conquest is not the conquest of force but the victory of love. What finally subdues a man is not that which breaks his strength by might, but that which breaks his heart by love. Jesus is the Lord of men, not because he was a conquering king, but because he was crucified upon a cross.

For self-examination: *do I in all my dealings with men take the way of love?*

THE STORY OF JOSEPH

GENESIS 37-50

We turn our attention to the story of Joseph. We do well to do so for two reasons. (1) It is one of the great stories of the world. There is nothing in history, or literature, or drama, to surpass it for sheer beauty and incident. It ranks with the literary masterpieces of the world. (2) There is no story which so sets out before us the lesson of the overruling providence of God. ''But as for you,' said Joseph to his brothers at the end of the day, ''you thought evil against me; but God meant it for good' (*Genesis* 50:20). Here again we learn the lesson that if we meet life in trust and fidelity to God, we shall at the end have cause to bless the hand that guided and the heart that planned.

THE SIN OF JEALOUSY

Genesis 37:1-4

> ¹Jacob dwelt in the land of his father's sojournings, in the land of Canaan. ²This is the history of the family of Jacob.
>
> Joseph, being seventeen years old, was shepherding the flock with his brothers; he was a lad with the sons of Bilhah and Zilpah, his father's wives; and Joseph brought an ill report of them to their father. ³ Now Israel loved Joseph more than any other of his children, because he was the son of his old age; and he made him a long robe with sleeves. ⁴But when his brothers saw that their father loved him more than all his brothers, they hated him, and could not speak peaceably to him.

The story of Joseph starts with one of the oldest sins in the world. It may be that Jacob was wrong to make his preference for Joseph so plain. It may be that Joseph was not altogether wise when he brought to his father the evil report of his brothers; but the brothers were wrong with their jealousy.

That jealousy poisoned the whole family circle. In the end it nearly broke Jacob's heart; it turned Joseph's brothers into murderers, in purpose, if not in fact; and it made Joseph an exile in a strange land.

The great trouble about jealousy is that it injures not only him who bears it and him against whom it is borne. It poisons every relationship of life and turns fellowship into enmity and love into suspicion.

A prayer: *O God, who loves all men, keep me from jealousy and envy. Make me ever to remember that I must not grudge to others what they have: but that I must do the best I can with what I myself possess to serve you and my fellow-men.*

THE CONSCIOUSNESS OF GREATNESS

Genesis 37: 5-11

> [5]Now Joseph had a dream, and when he told it to his brothers they only hated him the more. [6]He said to them, "Hear this dream which I have dreamed: [7]behold, we were binding sheaves in the field, and lo, my sheaf arose and stood upright; and behold, your sheaves gathered round it, and bowed down to my sheaf." [8]His brothers said to him, "Are you indeed to reign over us? Or are you indeed to have dominion over us?" So they hated him yet more for his dreams and for his words. [9]Then he dreamed another dream, and told it to his brothers, and said, "Behold, I have dreamed another dream; and behold, the sun, the moon, and eleven stars were bowing down to me." [10]But when he told it to his father and to his brothers, his father rebuked him, and said to him, "What is this dream that you have dreamed? Shall I and your mother and your brothers indeed come to bow ourselves to the ground before you?" [11]And his brothers were jealous of him, but his father kept the saying in mind.

The dreams of Joseph must not be taken as evidence of self-conceit and pride. They signify the sense of greatness which all great men have had. 'Great men come often; but the like of me comes once a century,' said John Knox. When Balzac, the writer, was contemplating a career in literature, his father tried to dissuade him by telling him that in writing there was no halfway house; a man would either become a beggar or a king. 'Very well then', answered the lad, 'I will become a king.'

But the sense of greatness which the truly great have, is not a sense of self-importance or a sense of their own strength. It is a sense of a task given them by God to do and the hand of God aiding them to do it. 'I can do all things,' said Paul, but he did not stop there. He went on to add, *'through Christ who strengthens me'* (*Phillipians* 4:13). Great men are dependent on God.

A prayer: *help me, O God, to put my trust in you, that no task may ever daunt me.*

A BOY'S OBEDIENCE

Genesis 37:12-17

¹²Now his brothers went to pasture their father's flock near Shechem. ¹³And Israel said to Joseph, "Are not your brothers pasturing the flock at Shechem? Come, I will send you to them." And he said to him, "Here I am." ¹⁴So he said to him, "Go now, see if it is well with your brothers, and with the flocks; and bring me word again." So he sent him from the valley of Hebron, and he came to Shechem. ¹⁵And a man found him wandering in the fields; and the man asked him, "What are you seeking?" ¹⁶"I am seeking my brothers," he said, "tell me, I pray you, where they are pasturing the flock." ¹⁷And the man said, "They have gone away, for I heard them say, 'Let us go to Dothan.' " So Joseph went after his brothers, and found them at Dothan.

Here is set out before us the obedience of Joseph. When his father summons him to a task, his answer is, 'Here am I.' His sense of greatness did not make him proud: it made him humble. Great as he knew his destiny to be, he served in humble obedience.

Jesus told us that he who would be greatest must be the servant of all. If we walk through some area devastated by war and, seeing the ruins, ask who was responsible for them, we may be told that some conquering general passed that way. If we journey through the middle west of America we shall see mile after mile of orchards; if we ask who planted all these orchards we shall learn of an old man called 'Johnny Appleseed', who in the old days walked about with a pocket full of appleseeds and scattered them wherever he went so that the orchards would grow. Should we like to be remembered as the man who brought the ruins, or the man who planted the orchards?

In the last analysis it is *historically true* that the servant — and the man of peace — is remembered as the great man.

To think about: *what is the motive of my life? Is it to serve or is it to rule? In my own home do I do things for others? Or do I keep other people doing things for me?*

REUBEN THE WEAK

Genesis 37:18-22,29-30

¹⁸They saw him afar off, and before he came near to them they conspired against him to kill him. ¹⁹They said to one another, "Here comes this dreamer. ²⁰Come now, let us kill him and throw him into one of the pits; then we shall say that a wild beast has devoured him, and we shall see what will become of his dreams." ²¹But when Reuben heard it, he delivered him out of their hands, saying, "Let us not take his life." ²²And Reuben said to them, "Shed no blood; cast him into this pit here in the wilderness, but lay no hand upon him" — that he might rescue him out of their hand, to restore him to his father. ...

²⁹When Reuben returned to the pit and saw that Joseph was not in the pit, he rent his clothes ³⁰and returned to his brothers, and said, "The lad is gone; and I, where shall I go?"

Here is Reuben the man of compromise. He knew how wrong it was to attack Joseph but he was afraid to come out into the open and defy his brothers to do their worst. He adopted a compromise which he hoped in the end would work out all right. But the compromise ended in disaster and left him lamenting.

The way of compromise is never the right way. It seeks to dispose of trouble by avoiding it. There is only one way to avoid trouble and that is by facing it. Conrad tells how when he was learning to steer a sailing ship, he was one day at the wheel in a storm. The old captain gave him one command over and over again: 'Keep her facing it; keep her facing it.' The way to ride out a storm is not to run away from it, but to face it.

For me: *is there any decision, any hard thing, from which I have been running away? Let me face it — now.*

OF TWO EVILS

Genesis 37:23-8

[23]So when Joseph came to his brothers, they stripped him of his robe, the long robe with sleeves that he wore; [24]and they took him and cast him into a pit. The pit was empty, there was no water in it.

[25]Then they sat down to eat; and looking up they saw a caravan of Ish'maelites coming from Gilead, with their camels bearing gum, balm, and myrrh, on their way to carry it down to Egypt. [26]Then Judah said to his brothers, "What profit is it if we slay our brother and conceal his blood? [27]Come, let us sell him to the Ish'maelites, and let not our hand be upon him, for he is our brother, our own flesh." And his brothers heeded him. [28]Then Mid'ianite traders passed by; and they drew Joseph up and lifted him out of the pit, and sold him to the Ish'maelites for twenty shekels of silver: and they took Joseph to Egypt.

Judah was faced with two evils. His brothers wished to kill Joseph. He wished to save him. The alternative seemed to be to sell him as a slave into Egypt. And he persuaded them so to do.

Judah thought he was choosing the lesser of two evils; and so he was; but as well as making an exile of his brother he was breaking his father's heart and making himself and his brothers guilty of a sinful deed.

We commonly say, of two evils choose the lesser. We ought to say, *of two evils choose neither*. In the last analysis there is only one way to the fulness of life; that is to choose not the middle path, but the right path and to abide in it to the end.

A prayer: *help me ever, O God, to choose the hard right and refuse the easy wrong.*

DECEPTION AND SORROW

Genesis 37:31-5

> [31]Then they took Joseph's robe, and killed a goat, and dipped the robe in the blood; [32]and they sent the long robe with sleeves and brought it to their father, and said: "This we have found: see now whether it is your son's robe or not." [33]And he recognized it, and said, "It is my son's robe; a wild beast has devoured him; Joseph is without doubt torn to pieces." [34]Then Jacob rent his garments, and put sackcloth upon his loins, and mourned for his son many days. [35]All his sons and all his daughters rose up to comfort him; but he refused to be comforted, and said, "No, I shall go down to Sheol to my son, mourning." Thus his father wept for him.

We have in this passage two things, the second inevitably following from the first.

First, we have deception. When a man commits a crime the first thing he tries to do is to put together some story that will save him from the consequences. Sin and falsehood inevitably and invariably go hand in hand.

But second, we have sorrow. Sooner or later, deception leads to the breaking of someone's heart. Surely one of the great defences against sin must be that, even if we do not worry about ruining our own life, we must stop and think before we bring sorrow to another's heart. Can we commit sin and afterwards meet the hurt and wounded look in someone's eyes?

It is one of the laws of life that we never sin only to ourselves. By sinning we injure and degrade ourselves — that is lamentable. By sinning we also bring sorrow and heartbreak to someone else — that is worse. And by sinning we bring grief to God — that is worst of all.

A prayer: *O God, keep us from bringing sorrow to others and grief to your heart of love. To those who have suffered grievously because of another's sin and foolishness, grant your strength and peace this day.*

A GOOD MAN'S SUCCESS

Genesis 39:1-6

¹Now Joseph was taken down to Egypt, and Pot'i-phar, an officer of Pharaoh, the captain of the guard, an Egyptian, bought him from the Ish'maelites who had brought him down there. ²The LORD was with Joseph, and he became a successful man; and he was in the house of his master the Egyptian, ³and his master saw that the LORD was with him, and that the LORD caused all that he did to prosper in his hands. ⁴So Joseph found favour in his sight and attended him, and he made him overseer of his house and put him in charge of all that he had. ⁵From the time that he made him overseer in his house and over all that he had the LORD blessed the Egyptian's house for Joseph's sake; the blessing of the LORD was upon all that he had, in house and field. ⁶So he left all that he had in Joseph's charge; and having him he had no concern for anything but the food which he ate.

So Joseph was sold in Egypt and became the slave of Potiphar, the captain of the king's guard. Then the wonderful thing happened — Joseph became to Potiphar so trusted a servant that Potiphar trusted him with his very life.

Two thoughts meet us here. First, it is clear that Joseph must have spent no time in useless repining and regret. He set to in the situation in which he found himself and made the best of it. Marshall Foch said that the whole art of war was to do the best you could with the resources you had. That also is the art of living, and Joseph was a master of that art.

But second, we are reminded that character always counts. Joseph arrived in Egypt a slave. No one knew who he was; yet by sheer force of character, by sheer fidelity, he raised himself from the ruck of men until he became a trusted servant of his master. The man who has the grace of God in his heart and the goodness of God in his life will succeed in gaining the respect of his fellow-men under any circumstances.

To think over today: *when I am caught up in some misfortune and when things go against me, do I waste my time in vain regrets? Am I mastered by my circumstances or do I master them? As Paul said (*Romans 8:37), *we can be more than conquerors through him that loved us! But do we honestly believe that?*

THE SLANDERER

Genesis 39:7-14

[7]And after a time his master's wife cast her eyes upon Joseph, and said "Lie with me." [8]But he refused and said to his master's wife, "Lo, having me my master has no concern about anything in the house, and he has put everything that he has in my hand; [9]he is not greater in this house than I am; nor has he kept back anything from me except yourself, because you are his wife; how then can I do this great wickedness, and sin against God?" [10]And although she spoke to Joseph day after day, he would not listen to her, to lie with her or to be with her. [11]But one day, when he went into the house to do his work and none of the men of the house was there in the house, [12]she caught him by his garment, saying, "Lie with me." But he left his garment in her hand, and fled and got out of the house. [13]And when she saw that he had left his garment in her hand, and had fled out of the house, [14] she called to the men of her household. ...

Joseph's misfortunes were not at an end. Potiphar's wife cast desirous eyes at him. Think what a temptation was brought to this young man. Trusted as he was, he was still a slave, and this lady of high degree was offering him what she thought was the honour of an intrigue with her. It took real strength of character to resist that.

Note Joseph's answer (v9). Two things kept Joseph from falling to temptation. One was that as a man of honour he would not betray a trust. He had been trusted by his master and he would not fail him. A man would never go far wrong if he insisted at all costs in being true to the trusts that have been reposed in him. For another thing, Joseph knew it would also be a sin against God. Sin against a fellow-man is always sin against God.

Now note that sin repulsed became malice in action. Potiphar's wife, her dishonourable approach refused, took a malicious revenge. It is strange but true that one sin leads to another. Let no man think, this once and then I will stop. He will find that the one wrong-doing leads to another, until sin has him in a grip from which — in his own strength — there is no escape.

A prayer: *O God of truth, keep me true to myself, true to my loved ones and true to you.*

To repeat during the day: *'Lead us not into temptation, but deliver us from evil.'*

GOD WITH HIM

Genesis 39:19-23

> [19]When his master heard the words which his wife spoke to him, "This is the way your servant treated me," his anger was kindled. [20]And Joseph's master took him and put him into the prison, the place where the king's prisoners were confined, and he was there in prison. [21]But the LORD was with Joseph and showed him steadfast love, and gave him favour in the sight of the keeper of the prison. [22]And the keeper of the prison committed to Joseph's care all the prisoners who were in the prison; and whatever was done there, he was the doer of it; [23]the keeper of the prison paid no heed to anything that was in Joseph's care, because the LORD was with him; and whatever he did, the LORD made it prosper.

Once again we find Joseph true to his character. He had suffered so much that might have driven him to despair and cynical indifference. He was an exile, and now in prison. His loyalty to the right had brought him to this. But Joseph's reaction was neither despair nor cynicism; he could serve God in a prison just as well as he could serve God as a free man.

Once again he took the simple, manly way. He did what his hand found to do with all his might. He showed himself even in prison a man of fidelity and honour; and he rose by that force of character to a position of trust.

Do we ever say, if only I was somewhere else, in other surroundings, among other people, I could serve God so much better? Our task is to let our light shine wherever God has set us and wherever life has brought us.

A prayer: *O God, help me so to live, that, wherever I am, my life may shine like a light in a dark place.*

The key to this passage: *'The Lord was with Joseph' (v21).*

THE DREAMS AND THE INTERPRETER

Genesis 40:1-8

[1]Some time after this, the butler of the king of Egypt and his baker offended their lord the king of Egypt. [2]And Pharaoh was angry with his two officers, the chief butler and the chief baker, [3]and he put them in custody in the house of the captain of the guard, in the prison where Joseph was confined. [4]The captain of the guard charged Joseph with them, and he waited on them; and they continued for some time in custody. [5]And one night they both dreamed — the butler and the baker of the king of Egypt, who were confined in the prison — each his own dream, and each dream with its own meaning. [6]When Joseph came to them in the morning and saw them, they were troubled. [7]So he asked Pharaoh's officers who were with him in custody in his master's house, ''Why are your faces downcast today''? [8]They said to him, ''We have had dreams, and there is no one to interpret them.'' And Joseph said to them, ''Do not interpretations belong to God? Tell them to me, I pray you.''

Dreams figure prominently in the story of Joseph. We must remember that we are reading a story of very primitive times, a story which goes back well before Christ came. In those ancient days, men believed that God spoke to them in dreams, that when a man's faculties were stilled and silenced in sleep, God came to him. So the butler and the baker dreamed dreams, and did not know what the dreams signified. 'We have dreamed a dream and there is no interpreter of it.'

Here we have a universal cry of the human heart. Men dream their dreams. They have a vision of themselves as the men they might be; or a vision of the world as it might be — and they are frustrated and irritated because they cannot interpret the dream. But 'interpretations belong to God'. There is only one interpreter of the dreams of men; for only in Christ can a man's vision of himself and of the world come true.

A prayer: *O Lord Jesus, take my life and mould and fashion it for yourself, that by your grace and your power my dreams may at last come true.*

THE DREAMS INTERPRETED

Genesis 40:9-19

⁹So the chief butler told his dream to Joseph, and said to him, "In my dream there was a vine before me, ¹⁰and on the vine there were three branches; as soon as it budded, its blossoms shot forth, and the clusters ripened into grapes. ¹¹Pharaoh's cup was in my hand; and I took the grapes and pressed them into Pharaoh's cup, and placed the cup in Pharaoh's hand." ¹²Then Joseph said to him, "This is its interpretation: the three branches are three days; ¹³within three days Pharaoh will lift up your head and restore you to your office; and you shall place Pharaoh's cup in his hand as formerly, when you were his butler. ¹⁴But remember me, when it is well with you, and do me the kindness, I pray you, to make some mention of me to Pharaoh, and so get me out of this house. ¹⁵For I was indeed stolen out of the land of the Hebrews; and here also I have done nothing that they should put me in the dungeon."

¹⁶When the chief baker saw that the interpretation was favourable, he said to Joseph, "I also had a dream: there were three cake baskets on my head, ¹⁷and in the uppermost basket there were all sorts of baked food for Pharaoh, but the birds were eating it out of the basket on my head." ¹⁸And Joseph answered, "This is its interpretation: the three baskets are three days; ¹⁹within three days Pharaoh will lift up your head — from you! — and hang you on a tree; and the birds will eat the flesh from you."

So the two dreams were told to Joseph and he with the skill God had given him, gave the butler the interpretation of good and the baker the interpretation of evil.

Once again, Joseph is true to his character. First, he told the truth. It would have been much easier to give the baker the kind of interpretation he wanted, but Joseph told him the truth, hard as it was. 'You have sought to kill me,' Jesus once said, 'a man who has told you the truth.' The Christian must have a certain uncompromising quality in him when it comes to speaking the truth.

Second, all that Joseph asked by way of reward was that the butler when he should be released should remember him to Pharaoh. Joseph wanted a chance to make good. He was conscious of his own innocence, and he did not fear a fair trial. He wanted no reward other than to be set free and to find fresh opportunities for service.

For meditation: *am I ever afraid to speak the truth? Would I welcome a trial, conscious of my own innocence, or are there things I wish to hide?*

MAN'S INGRATITUDE

Genesis 40:20-23

[20]On the third day, which was Pharaoh's birthday, he made a feast for all his servants, and lifted up the head of the chief butler and the head of the chief baker among his servants. [21]He restored the chief butler to his butlership, and he placed the cup in Pharaoh's hand; [22]but he hanged the chief baker, as Joseph had interpreted to them. [23]Yet the chief butler did not remember Joseph, but forgot him.

The interpretations which Joseph had given came true. The butler was restored to his place of honour.

In verse 23, with that economy of words so characteristic of scripture, there comes the simple, yet poignant, statement: 'Yet the chief butler did not remember Joseph, but forgot him.' Surely one of the sorest things in life is man's ingratitude. So often the child is ungrateful to the parent, forgetting all the countless things he has received. So often friend is ungrateful to friend, forgetting his friend's help and support when the day of need is past. So often men are ungrateful to God, forgetting that God so loved the world that he gave for us — *for me* — his only son.

A prayer: *I thank you, O Father, for all your gifts to me: grant me one gift more — the grateful heart.*

When all Thy mercies, O my God,
My rising soul surveys,
Transported with the view, I'm lost
In wonder, love and praise.

THE KING'S DREAMS

Genesis 41:1-8

¹After two whole years, Pharaoh dreamed that he was standing by the Nile, ²and behold, there came up out of the Nile seven cows, sleek and fat, and they fed in the reed grass. ³And behold, seven other cows, gaunt and thin, came up out of the Nile after them, and stood by the other cows on the bank of the Nile. ⁴And the gaunt and thin cows ate up the seven sleek and fat cows. And Pharaoh awoke. ⁵And he fell asleep and dreamed a second time; and behold, seven ears of grain, plump and good, were growing on one stalk. ⁶And behold, after them sprouted seven ears, thin and blighted by the east wind. ⁷And the thin ears swallowed up the seven plump and full ears. And Pharaoh awoke, and behold, it was a dream. ⁸So in the morning his spirit was troubled; and he sent and called for all the magicians of Egypt and all its wise men; and Pharaoh told them his dream, but there was none who could interpret it to Pharaoh.

Pharaoh's dreams were vivid. He saw the lean cows devour the fat cows, and the full ears swallowed up by the thin ears; but the wise men of Egypt failed to read these dreams.

Now it is true that God sends his warnings and foretellings to men. But it is also true that it takes a man of God to read the signs aright. Only one whose heart is attuned to God and whose spirit is akin to the Spirit of God can understand what God is saying. May it not be that, when we find life a mystery, it is because we do not live close enough to God to understand the signs he sends? May it not be that, when we stand at some crossroads and know not which way to take, it is because we are not attuned to God as we ought to be and because we have listened so long to the voices of the world that we do not recognise the voice of God?

Certain it is that if we lived closer to God many dark places would be lighted and many mysteries would be made plain.

A prayer: *help me, O God, to live so close to you that I may ever say, take my hand and lead me on.*

Think about this today: *we can read the signs of the weather. Are we sufficiently on the watch for signs of God's presence and God's activity?*

REMEMBERED IN TROUBLE

Genesis 41:9-13

[9]Then the chief butler said to Pharaoh, "I remember my faults today. [10]When Pharaoh was angry with his servants, and put me and the chief baker in custody in the house of the captain of the guard, [11]we dreamed on the same night, he and I, each having a dream with its own meaning. [12]A young Hebrew was there with us, a servant of the captain of the guard; and when we told him, he interpreted our dreams to us, giving an interpretation to each man according to his dream. [13]And as he interpreted to us, so it came to pass; I was restored to my office, and the baker was hanged."

In Pharaoh's bewilderment and perplexity, the chief butler remembered the young stranger who had interpreted his own dreams. For a time he had forgotten Joseph, but now he remembered.

There is something here that is typical of human nature. It is characteristic of many of us that we remember our friends when things go badly, and forget them when things go well. In other words, we remember them when we need them. Or, to put it in plainer language still, we remember them chiefly when we hope to get something out of them! It is a fine thing to feel that there is someone to whom we can go when we are in trouble and be sure of their sympathy and help. That is the very essence of friendship; but how selfish it is only to remember people when we need them.

And that is what so many of us do with God. When we are in trouble, or sickness or sorrow, or in time of war, then we pray; but when the crisis is past and things are going easily again we conveniently forget about God. In fair days and foul, we should keep our friendships in constant repair. In the dark, and in the light, we should walk with God day by day.

A prayer: *O God, I know that I am often driven to my knees in prayer because I have nowhere else to go: but help me to speak with you also when things go well, and help me to make my prayer-life constant.*

GOD SHALL GIVE AN ANSWER

Genesis 41:14-16

> [14]Then Pharaoh sent and called Joseph, and they brought him hastily out of the dungeon; and when he had shaved himsef and changed his clothes, he came in before Pharaoh. [15]And Pharaoh said to Joseph, "I have had a dream, and there is no one who can interpret it; and I have heard it said of you that when you hear a dream you can interpret it". [16]Joseph answered Pharaoh, "It is not in me; God will give Pharaoh a favourable answer."*

So Joseph was brought to find an answer to the perplexing dreams.

Note his answer in verse 16. 'It is not in me; God shall give Pharaoh an answer.' Here was a chance in a million for Joseph to glorify himself and to give the impression that out of his own wisdom and skill he could give Pharaoh an interpretation. But Joseph gave the glory to God.

Herein we have two of the great secrets of Joseph's life. First, his humility. Joseph might have been tempted to acquire power and use it selfishly. But life for him was one long opportunity to serve others and to serve God.

Second, we note what we may call his God-dependence. Joseph met the tragedies and tests of life not in his own strength, but in the strength he drew from God. The old Greeks used to have a tale about the Locrian Ajax, who, being shipwrecked, refused to pray or ask for help from the gods, whereat, when he thought he was saving himself, Poseidon the sea god blasted him with a thunderbolt. There is this much truth in the old tale; that the man who says he can deal with life in his own strength is on the sure road to disaster.

Let me examine myself: *am I ever guilty of the self-confidence which leaves God out of the reckoning?*

*Verse 16 in Dr Moffat's translation: 'Not I!' said Joseph to the Pharaoh; 'it is God's answer that will answer to the Pharaoh.'

THE PRACTICAL MAN

Genesis 41:25,33-6

> ^{25}Then Joseph said to Pharaoh, "The dream of Pharaoh is one; God has revealed to Pharaoh what he is about to do. ...^{33}Now therefore let Pharaoh select a man discreet and wise, and set him over the land of Egypt. ^{34}Let Pharaoh proceed to appoint overseers over the land, and take the fifth part of the produce of the land of Egypt during the seven plenteous years. ^{35}And let them gather all the food of these good years that are coming, and lay up grain under the authority of Pharaoh for food in the cities, and let them keep it. ^{36}That food shall be a reserve for the land against the seven years of famine which are to befall the land of Egypt, so that the land may not perish through the famine."

Joseph told Pharaoh the meaning of his dreams that the seven fat cattle and the seven fat ears were seven good years; that the seven lean cattle and the seven thin ears were evil years; and that the fact that the lean were to swallow up the fat meant that a great famine was on the way.

It is never easy to be the bearer of bad tidings; and it can be especially dangerous to bear bad tidings to a king. Once again we see Joseph without fear or favour telling *the truth*. Once that great Scot Andrew Melville wrote something uncomplimentary about the royal house of Scotland in one of his books. He was told that it would certainly get him into trouble. 'Is it true?' he asked. His friends admitted it was true. 'Then,' said Melville, 'let it stand.' He stood by the truth.

But the outstanding thing about Joseph here is that he could not only diagnose a situation; *he knew the way to deal with it*. There are any number of voices that can tell us what is wrong; there are few who can tell us what to do about it! The man of God must never be satisfied with purely destructive criticism; he must go on to tell men what God wants done to meet the situation.

A prayer: *O God, give me not only understanding to know, but courage to act.*

JOSEPH THE PRIME MINISTER

Genesis 41:37-43

[37]This proposal seemed good to Pharaoh and to all his servants. [38]And Pharaoh said to his servants, "Can we find such a man as this, in whom is the Spirit of God?" [39]So Pharaoh said to Joseph, "Since God has shown you all this, there is none so discreet and wise as you are; [40]you shall be over my house, and all my people shall order themselves as you command; only as regards the throne will I be greater than you." [41]And Pharaoh said to Joseph, "Behold, I have set you over all the land of Egypt." [42]Then Pharaoh took his signet ring from his hand and put it on Joseph's hand, and arrayed him in garments of fine linen, and put a gold chain about his neck; [43]and he made him to ride in his second chariot; and they cried before him, "Bow the knee!" Thus he set him over all the land of Egypt.

No other incident shows so well the sheer force of Joseph's character and the strength of his personality. It is an amazing thing that Joseph should come into Pharaoh's presence a prisoner and leave it as prime minister.

Verse 42 speaks of Pharaoh giving Joseph his ring. In the ancient world, to give a man your signet ring was to invest him with every power which you yourself had. Joseph was put into supreme command of the kingdom of Egypt.

Note the qualities of Joseph which so impressed Pharaoh in verse 39. Joseph was discreet and wise. It is only when those two qualities are combined that a man becomes great. A man may have so much discretion that he is ultimately incapable of action at all; or a man may be very clever, yet because he lacks discretion his cleverness becomes a handicap to himself and a danger to other people. A man must have both intellectual and moral force.

The danger into which the world has now run is that man's intellect has acquired a power over the secrets of nature which he is not morally fit to use. How fine and prosperous life might be if we handled aright our knowledge. Never did the world need more Christian men and women than today.

A prayer: *O God, so fill me with your Spirit that I may use my every power and my every talent in accordance with your will.*

THE MAN WHO KNEW

Genesis 41:50-57

[50]Before the year of famine came, Joseph had two sons, whom As'enath, the daughter of Poti'phera priest of On, bore to him. [51]Joseph called the name of the first-born Manas'seh, "For," he said, "God has made me forget all my hardship and all my father's house." [52]The name of the second he called E'phraim, "For God has made me fruitful in the land of my affliction."

[53]The seven years of plenty that prevailed in the land of Egypt came to an end; [54]and the seven years of famine began to come, as Joseph had said. There was famine in all lands; but in all the land of Egypt there was bread. [55]When all the land of Egypt was famished, the people cried to Pharaoh for bread; and Pharaoh said to all the Egyptians, "Go to Joseph; what he says to you, do." [56]So when the famine had spread over all the land, Joseph opened all the store-houses, and sold to the Egyptians, for the famine was severe in the land of Egypt. [57]Moreover, all the earth came to Egypt to Joseph to buy grain, because the famine was severe over all the earth.

Joseph, in the land of his exile, found himself a wife and begat children. Note how even in the naming of his children Joseph expresses his gratitude to God. Adversity can test a man: but prosperity is a still greater test. Many come through adversity with colours flying, yet fall to the subtler temptations, to pride and self-confidence which prosperity brings.

Note what Pharaoh told the people when the famine descended upon the land. 'Go to Joseph; what he says to you, do' (v55). In the emergency Joseph was the one man who could tell people what to do.

As we read in the gospels, we find bewildered people coming to Jesus and asking, what am I to do about life and about myself? And Jesus told them. The follower of Jesus must be like his Master. If Christians were really carrying out their function in the world they would have such wisdom of mind, such strength of character, such winsomeness of personality, that they would be the guides and counsellors of all.

To think over: *in an emergency — at home, in my work or profession, in the street, or in a national emergency — am I prepared to be an asset or a liability? If possible read the story of St Paul's shipwreck in Acts 27: It is an outstanding example of how a Christian man towered above everyone else in a desperate crisis.*

51

THE MEETING

Genesis 42:1-2, 6-8

[1]When Jacob learned that there was grain in Egypt, he said to his sons, "Why do you look at one another?" [2]And he said, "Behold, I have heard that there is grain in Egypt; go down and buy grain for us there, that we may live, and not die. ..." [6]Now Joseph was governor over the land; he it was who sold to all the people of the land. And Joseph's brothers came, and bowed themselves before him with their faces to the ground. [7]Joseph saw his brothers, and knew them, but he treated them like strangers and spoke roughly to them. "Where do you come from?" he said. They said, "From the land of Canaan, to buy food." [8]Thus Joseph knew his brothers, but they did not know him.

There was famine all over Egypt; and it extended to the land where Jacob and his family lived. Everyone knew there was corn in Egypt, so Jacob sent his sons there to buy corn; however, warned by what had happened to Joseph, he did not send Benjamin, his youngest and dearest son.

So the brothers came to Egypt. Now there comes a dramatic moment. 'And Joseph knew his brethren, but they knew him not' (v8). The years had passed by and they did not recognise the dazzling figure of the prime minister as the lad they had once sold as a slave.

Surely of all the tests that ever came to Joseph this was the most searching. He had proved himself in adversity; he had proved himself in prosperity. Now he had to answer the question, 'Will I take vengeance? Or will I forgive?'

Suppose the man who has wronged you, the man whom you have every cause to hate, were suddenly to be placed in your power, what would you do with him? How many of us would survive such a test as that? Yet think of God. How deeply we have hurt God and still he loves us with a love that will not let us go. We also, however faintly, must be like that.

Consider the words of Jesus in *Matthew* 18: 34-5, which conclude the story of the unforgiving servant. We all know people who have afflicted upon themselves 'a living hell' because they refused to forgive a wrong done to them.

A prayer: *Lord, grant me a forgiving spirit.*

JOSEPH'S TEST

Genesis 42:9-15

[9]And Joseph remembered the dreams which he had dreamed of them; and he said to them, "You are spies, you have come to see the weakness of the land." [10]They said to him, "No, my lord, but to buy food have your servants come. [11]We are all sons of one man, we are honest men, your servants are not spies." [12]He said to them, "No, it is the weakness of the land that you have come to see." [13] And they said, "We, your servants, are twelve brothers, the sons of one man in the land of Canaan; and behold, the youngest is this day with our father, and one is no more." [14]But Joseph said to them, "It is as I said to you, you are spies. [15]By this you shall be tested: by the life of Pharaoh, you shall not go from this place unless your youngest brother comes here.

There was no vindictiveness in Joseph. He sought not to revenge himself but to forgive; but he knew human nature. He knew that a forgiveness too easily earned, a forgiveness which seems indifferently to condone sin, may do more harm than good to the person forgiven. Joseph's aim is not to bring unnecessary pain to his brothers and to play a cat-and-mouse game with them, but to awaken them again to the seriousness of the crime they had once committed.

So he accused them of being spies and they indignantly denied it. But notice what they say; there are twelve brothers (their youngest is still at home) — 'and one is not' (v13). They cannot forget their sin. That is always the penalty of sin. We are so constructed that we cannot sin in peace. If even at the moment there are no qualms or regrets in our minds, memories will come. The brothers were haunted by the thought of the one who, through their fault, was not. Let no man ever think that an act of sin will bring happiness, for once a man sins he forfeits his peace of heart.

So the story unfolds. Joseph insisted that their youngest brother must come or he would not believe their story, and one of them must remain as a hostage.

A prayer: *O God, most merciful, save me from doing anything which will bring bitter memories.*

THE STING OF CONSCIENCE

Genesis 42:21-4

[21]Then they said to one another, "In truth we are guilty concerning our brother, in that we saw the distress of his soul, when he besought us and we would not listen; therefore is this distress come upon us." [22]And Reuben answered them, "Did I not tell you not to sin against the lad? But you would not listen. So now there comes a time for reckoning for his blood." [23]They did not know that Joseph understood them, for there was an interpreter between them. [24]Then he turned away from them and wept; and he returned to them and spoke to them. And he took Simeon from them and bound him before their eyes.

Again, there is drama here. As the brothers talked in the Hebrew tongue they little thought that the man they took for an Egyptian prince could understand what they were saying.

How near the surface of their minds was the consciousness of their sin. Instinctively they connected their present plight with their past sin. Hear Reuben speak. He is saying weakly, 'I told you so.' Had he not taken the way of compromise instead of principle on that fateful day years before, he might well have prevented the unhappy deed. The brothers are discovering that sooner or later a man's sin will find him out.

So Simeon was bound and kept as a hostage.

A prayer: *when I am tempted, O God, give me strength to stand firm so that I shall not be haunted by shame and sorrow.*

AN OLD MAN'S SORROW

Genesis 42: 25-6, 36-8

> [25]And Joseph gave orders to fill their bags with grain, and to replace every man's money in his sack, and to give them provisions for the journey. This was done for them.
>
> [26]Then they loaded their asses with their grain, and departed. … [36]And Jacob their father said to them, "You have bereaved me of my children: Joseph is no more, and Simeon is no more, and now you would take Benjamin; all this has come upon me." [37]Then Reuben said to his father, "Slay my two sons if I do not bring him back to you; put him in my hands, and I will bring him back to you." [38]But he said, "My son shall not go down with you, for his brother is dead, and he only is left. If harm should befall him on the journey that you are to make, you would bring down my grey hairs with sorrow to Sheol."

Although Joseph knew his brothers must realise the seriousness of their past sin, there was kindness in his heart. So he put back in their sacks of corn the money they had brought. They went home and told their story; they related to Jacob how Simeon was in prison in Egypt and would remain there until Benjamin was brought to the Pharaoh's prime minister.

The news went like a sword to Jacob's heart. Here one thing is borne in upon us — the long arm of sin. If we could sin and be done with it, even if it meant taking our punishment here and now, it would not be so terrible. But a sin committed years ago may send its shadow down the years. The sorrow was still fresh in Jacob's heart; and it seemed that a new sorrow was to be brought to him. The old evil deed was still casting its shadow on that household.

Read verse 37. But a man who has once failed in a trust is not likely to be trusted again. Reuben, the eldest son, had failed before, and Jacob would not trust him now. He did not know the real details of Reuben's conduct at the selling of Joseph, but he knew that the son who had the duty of bringing his younger brother safe home had failed to do so; and he could not bring himself to trust him again. That is often a penalty we have to suffer if we fail; but God is great-hearted enough to trust us again on the field of our defeat.

A prayer: *if ever I am tempted to sin, give me, O God, grace to pause and to think what this will mean for others, and especially for those I love, in the years to come.*

JACOB'S RESIGNATION

Genesis 43:1-14

> [1]Now the famine was severe in the land. [2]And when they had eaten the grain which they had brought from Egypt, their father said to them, ''Go again, buy us a little food.'' [3]But Judah said to him, ''The man solemnly warned us, saying, ''You shall not see my face, unless your brother is with you.'' ...
>
> [11]Then their father Israel said to them, ''If it must be so, then do this: take some of the choice fruits of the land in your bags, and carry down to the man a present, a little balm and a little honey, gum, myrrh, pistachio nuts, and almonds. [12]Take double the money with you; carry back with you the money that was returned in the mouth of your sacks; perhaps it was an oversight. [13]Take also your brother, and arise, go again to the man; [14]may God Almighty grant you mercy before the man, that he may send back your other brother and Benjamin. If I am bereaved of my children, I am bereaved.''

The pitiless impact of the famine once again drove Jacob and his household to need. Hunger is a master who will not be denied. So Judah offered to take upon himself the responsibility for the safe return of Benjamin if only Jacob would let him go. Observe now the resignation of Jacob. 'If it must be so now, do this' (v11); 'If I be bereaved of my children, I am bereaved' (v14).

Once Mr Asquith, as he then was, the famous prime minister, was rejected by a constituency which he had served well. His wife was almost afraid to go into his room to speak to him in face of this crushing blow. But she found him calm and serene. 'I have learned,' he said, 'to make my peace with events.'

Yet there are two kinds of resignation. There is the resignation of a man who feels himself helpless in the grip of a heartless fate. And there is the resignation of the man who feels himself, in the last analysis, in the hands of God. It was the second kind that Jacob had learned, for in verse 14 he commits the matter to God. It was that resignation that Jesus expressed when he said, 'Not my will, but yours be done.' May we also have that resignation, knowing that the everlasting arms are underneath and about us and those we love.

A prayer: *O God, teach me to commit my ways to you.*

GOD'S DOING

Genesis 43:15, 19-23

¹⁵So the men took the present, and they took double the money with them, and Benjamin; and they arose and went down to Egypt, and stood before Joseph. ... ¹⁹So they went up to the steward of Joseph's house, and spoke with him at the door of the house, ²⁰and said, "Oh, my lord, we came down the first time to buy food; ²¹and when we came to the lodging place we opened our sacks, and there was every man's money in the mouth of his sack, our money in full weight; so we have brought it again with us, ²²and we have brought other money down in our hand to buy food. We do not know who put our money in our sacks."²³He replied, "Rest assured, do not be afraid; your God and the God of your father must have put treasure in your sacks for you; I received your money." Then he brought Simeon out to them.

When the brothers reached Egypt they were almost terrified by the kindness with which they were received. There is nothing which can conquer a man like the power of kindness.

But in this passage there is a very wonderful thing. In verse 23 the steward speaks of 'your God and the God of your father.' The steward was an Egyptian, and must have been brought up in the worship of the Egyptian gods. He cannot have known in his early years about Yahweh the God of the Hebrews; yet here he is ascribing events to his power. How can that be? There can only be one reason. Joseph must have told him of the God of the Hebrews.

Here then we have still another great fact about Joseph. Even in exile, when things had gone so well that he might have forgotten God, in a strange land where he might well have conformed to the practices and customs of the people among whom he lived, Joseph was still a witness and a missionary for God. What a tremendous lesson. The Christian must never conform to the world. Even if he is set in a pagan society he must still bear his Christian witness and never be ashamed to show whose he is and whom he serves.

A prayer: *O God, help me always to be a witness and a missionary for you.*

For further thought: *'Your God,* and the God of your father' (v23). *It is a strangely uplifting thought that our God is the God in whom our fathers trusted. Many of them staked their all on him. 'God of our fathers, be the God of their succeeding race.'*

THE BOND OF KINSHIP

Genesis 43:26-31

[26]When Joseph came home, they brought into the house to him the present which they had with them, and bowed down to him to the ground. [27]And he inquired about their welfare, and said, ''Is your father well, the old man of whom you spoke? Is he still alive?''[28]They said, ''Your servant our father is well, he is still alive.'' And they bowed their heads, and made obeisance. [29]And he lifted up his eyes, and saw his brother Benjamin, his mother's son, and said, ''Is this your youngest brother, of whom you spoke to me? God be gracious to you, my son!'' [30]Then Joseph made haste, for his heart yearned for his brother, and he sought a place to weep. And he entered his chamber and wept there. [31]Then he washed his face and came out; and controlling himself he said, ''Let food be served.''

Surely this is the most human of all passages in the story of Joseph. How he longs for news of Jacob, his father! How he yearns with love over the young Benjamin. The years have not diminished the strength of the unbreakable bond of kindred and blood.

Sometimes when a man, as we say, gets on in the world, he is half ashamed of the stock from which he has come and is embarrassed by the sight of old friends and comrades. Not so Joseph. The years brought him almost royal power; but still in his heart is the love of home and family.

True it is that if a man is not loyal to his own, he will not be loyal to anyone else.

A prayer: *O God, who has set the solitary in families, help me to honour my family ties.*

BENJAMIN

Genesis 44:1-5

> [1]Then he commanded the steward of his house, "Fill the men's sacks with food, as much as they can carry, and put each man's money in the mouth of his sack, [2]and put my cup, the silver cup, in the mouth of the sack of the youngest, with his money for the grain." And he did as Joseph told him. [3]As soon as the morning was light, the men were sent away with their asses. [4]When they had gone but a short distance from the city, Joseph said to his steward, "Up, follow after the men; and when you overtake them, say to them, 'Why have you returned evil for good? Why have you stolen my silver cup? [5]Is it not from this that my lord drinks, and by this that he divines? You have done wrong in so doing.'"

Joseph's plan was maturing. He was going to teach these brothers of his a lesson they would never forget. He treated them with all kindness and generosity and sent them away. But in the sack of Benjamin he had put his own silver cup. The steward was sent in pursuit, and the cup was found.

Note again that the intensity of this new tragedy was doubled by the memory of the old sin. The possibility of the fate of Benjamin must have re-awakened in the minds of the brothers the fate of Joseph so many years before. They felt that they were caught up in a situation which was inexorably working itself out. That is precisely what sin always does. When a man sins, he sets in motion a train of events which in the end can only finish in tragedy. There is a law of righteousness in the universe which a man breaks only at his peril.

To think about: *Froude the historian said that across the centuries history proclaims one lesson — that* in the end *it is well with the good and ill with the wicked.*

JUDAH'S OFFER

Genesis 44:18, 30-34

> [18]Then Judah went up to him and said, "O my lord, let your servant, I pray you, speak a word in my lord's ears, and let not your anger burn against your servant; for you are like Pharaoh himself. ... [30]Now therefore, when I come to your servant my father, and the lad is not with us, then, as his life is bound up in the lad's life, [31]when he sees that the lad is not with us, he will die; and your servants will bring down the grey hairs of your servant our father with sorrow to Sheol. [32]For your servant became surety for the lad to my father, saying, 'If I do not bring him back to you, then I shall bear the blame in the sight of my father all my life.' [33]Now therefore, let your servant, I pray you, remain instead of the lad as a slave to my lord; and let the lad go back with his brothers. [34]For how can I go back to my father if the lad is not with me? I fear to see the evil that would come upon my father."

It was Judah who had been instrumental in saving Joseph's life, even if it had been at the cost of selling him as a slave. Now he offers his life for the life of Benjamin. There is nobility here. Surely we see at least a faint forecast of things to come. David was of the tribe of Judah; and Jesus was the Son of David. After long centuries had passed, in God's good time his Son came into the world and he came — according to the flesh — from the line of this man who offered his life for his brother's.

Nothing moves our hearts like the story of such an offer. Sacrifice is the greatest thing in life.

But there is another side to Judah's speech. Read verse 28. He is keeping something back. Even now he will not say, I and my brothers have sinned. He still attempts to conceal the dark deed that once he and his brothers did. Again it is but simple truth that there is no real peace for us until we confess our misdeeds to God and to the person we have wronged.

A prayer: *O God, give me Judah's spirit of sacrifice: but save me from making the mistake of trying to hide anything from you.*

RECOGNITION

Genesis 45:1-5

[1]Then Joseph could not control himself before all those who stood by him; and he cried "Make every one go out from me." So no one stayed with him when Joseph made himself known to his brothers. [2]And he wept aloud, so that the Egyptians heard it, and the household of Pharaoh heard it. [3]And Joseph said to his brothers, "I am Joseph; is my father still alive?" But his brothers could not answer him, for they were dismayed at his presence. [4]So Joseph said to his brothers, "Come near to me, I pray you." And they came near. And he said "I am your brother, Joseph, whom you sold into Egypt. [5]And now do not be distressed, or angry with yourselves, because you sold me here; for God sent me before you to preserve life. ..."

This has been called, and rightly so, the greatest recognition scene in literature. Suddenly the brothers are confronted with the brother whom they had so cruelly wronged.

First, think of the reaction of the brothers: fear. All they can think of is that the brother whom they wronged is now in a position to take vengeance upon them.

But second, there is the reaction of Joseph. 'You sold me here ... God sent me'. No doubt in the long years Joseph had thought about life. He had wondered why these things should have happened to him; and in the end he could only see one reason: it was all in the plan of God, and with that he was content.

When a man becomes utterly dependent on God he becomes utterly independent of men, because he knows that nothing that men can do with him will deflect the plan that God has for him. When he makes that great discovery, he is secure in the certainty that all things work together for good.

Then look at Joseph's further reaction. It is to share his good fortune with his father *and his brothers.* Joseph had reached the highest peak of human conduct — he had learned to return good for evil, and love for hatred.

It is said that the Old Testament is a hard book and that it teaches the doctrine of an eye for an eye and a tooth for a tooth. And so in some places it does. But here in the person of Joseph it rises far above that until we see the foreshadowing of the love of God in Christ.

A prayer: *O God, help me to see in everything that happens to me the guiding of your hand.*

AN OLD MAN'S JOY

Genesis 45:16-27

> [16]When the report was heard in Pharaoh's house, "Joseph's brothers have come," it pleased Pharaoh and his servants well. [17]And Pharaoh said to Joseph, "Say to your brothers, 'Do this: load your beasts and go back to that land of Canaan; [18]and take your father and your households, and come to me, and I will give you the best of the land of Egypt, and you shall eat the fat of the land.' ... [24] Then he sent his brothers away, and as they departed, he said to them, "Do not quarrel on the way." [25]So they went up out of Egypt, and came to the land of Canaan to their father Jacob. [26]And they told him, "Joseph is still alive, and he is ruler over all the land of Egypt." And his heart fainted, for he did not believe them. [27]But when they told him all the words of Joseph, which he had said to them, and when he saw the wagons which Joseph had sent to carry him, the spirit of their father Jacob revived. ...

Nothing can show better the relationship in which Joseph stood to Pharaoh than that Joseph's joy was Pharaoh's joy. Pharaoh was moved to great generosity to the family of the prime minister on whom he depended and whom he had come to hold in love.

There is a curiously human touch in verse 27. To Jacob the news seemed far too good to be true. The son whom he had mourned, but whom he could never forget, was said to be still alive. The old man at first was quite unable to believe it. Then 'when he saw the wagons' he believed.

It is true to life. Words always require the backing of deeds before they become alive. Jacob might have disbelieved a verbal message, but when he saw the proofs of Joseph's love and desire for him he could not but believe.

Joseph was alive; and Jacob felt now that life had no more to offer him. It is strangely true that in the end everything comes to him who waits in quiet trust in God. It may not come in the form he expects it. It may not come in the concrete way it came to Jacob. But he who trusts in God will not be confounded.

A prayer: *give me patience, O God, to wait upon you.*

GOD'S GUIDING HAND

Genesis 46:1-7

[1]So Israel took his journey with all that he had, and came to Beer-sheba, and offered sacrifices to the God of his father Isaac. [2]And God spoke to Israel in visions of the night, and said, "Jacob, Jacob." And he said, "Here am I". [3]Then he said "I am God, the God of your father; do not be afraid to go down to Egypt; for I will there make of you a great nation. [4]I will go down with you to Egypt, and I will also bring you up again; and Joseph's hand shall close your eyes." [5]Then Jacob set out from Beer-sheba; and the sons of Israel carried Jacob their father, their little ones, and their wives, in the wagons which Pharaoh had sent to carry him. [6]They also took their cattle and their goods, which they had gained in the land of Canaan, and came into Egypt, Jacob and all his offspring with him, [7]his sons, and his sons' sons with him, his daughters, and his sons' daughters; all his offspring he brought with him into Egypt.

It might well have been that one so advanced in years might have hesitated to make the long journey to Egypt. But God spoke to Jacob.

There is no doubt that this is one of the most important journeys in history. It led to the long stay of the children of Israel in Egypt; to the Egyptian bondage; to the Passover Feast which was the forerunner of our sacrament; to the work of Moses; and to the entrance of the promised land. It was a journey which profoundly influenced all human history to come.

So we have to note two things. First, one man's decision can literally affect a whole world. Jacob's decision to go to Egypt was an integral piece of the plan of God which led to the coming of Jesus Christ. There is no decision we can ever make which only affects ourselves.

Second, note Jacob's response to God. At the summons, Jacob answered, 'Here am I' (v2). Here is the perfect obedience. Jacob was old, but he was still prepared to do what God commanded. God offered him an adventure, and Jacob in his old age took it, so gaining an honoured place in the plan of God. God still needs those who are adventurous enough to respond to his call, even if obedience means an unknown road.

For meditation: *when God calls me, do I answer, here I am, or do I try to evade the tasks he has for me to do?*

THE HAPPY ENDING

Genesis 46:28-30

> [28]He sent Judah before him to Joseph, to appear before him in Goshen; and they came into the land of Goshen. [29]Then Joseph made ready his chariot and went up to meet Israel his father in Goshen; and he presented himself to him, and fell on his neck and wept on his neck a good while. [30]Israel said to Joseph, "Now let me die, since I have seen your face and know that you are still alive."

Here again with that noble economy of words the bible tells of the meeting of Joseph and his father, Jacob. In that meeting, sorrow and grief were swallowed up in the joy of reunion.

Surely such an incident turns our thoughts far beyond time, even to eternity. We live in a world of partings; but our eyes are turned to a land of reunions. God grant to us and to those we love that fidelity which will win us that meeting in the presence of God when life's partings are ended.

A prayer: *O God, when I am parted from my dear ones, help me beyond the sorrow of separation to glimpse the joy of being reunited.*

A NEW LIFE

Genesis 47:1-2, 5-7

¹So Joseph went in and told Pharaoh, "My father and my brothers, with their flocks and herds and all that they possess, have come from the land of Canaan; they are now in the land of Goshen." ²And from among his brothers he took five men and presented them to Pharaoh. ... ⁵Then Pharaoh said to Joseph "Your father and your brothers have come to you. ⁶The land of Egypt is before you; settle your father and your brothers in the best of the land; let them dwell in the land of Goshen; and if you know any able men among them, put them in charge of my cattle."

⁷Then Joseph brought in Jacob his father, and set him before Pharaoh, and Jacob blessed Pharaoh.

We have already seen that when Joseph was reunited to his family Pharaoh shared Joseph's joy. Now we see him extending the hospitality of his kingdom to Jacob and his family. And we see him doing reverence to Jacob's old age and honouring a venerable patriarch.

This is surprising. Why should the king of Egypt welcome with such open arms these strangers whom he did not know and who had come from afar? Why did he even without knowing them suggest that some of them at least should be installed straight away in places of responsibility and trust (v6)? The answer is clear. Pharaoh treated Joseph's brothers in this way *because he knew Joseph*. He said to himself, 'These men are of the same family as Joseph and if they are like him they are good men.' Joseph was the finest of advertisements for the family from which he came and for the faith which he held.

Here is a lesson for us. If we are to commend Christianity to the world — and it is our plain duty to do so — we shall not do it merely by our words, but by our deeds and our example. We must so live that men looking at us will be compelled to say that if Christianity enables a man to live like that, there must be something in it of surpassing value.

For meditation:*is my life a good example and a good advertisement for Christianity?*

THE CALL OF HOME

Genesis 47:27-31

²⁷Thus Israel dwelt in the land of Egypt, in the land of Goshen; and they gained possessions in it, and were fruitful and multiplied exceedingly. ²⁸And Jacob lived in the land of Egypt seventeen years; so the days of Jacob, the years of his life, were a hundred and forty-seven years.

²⁹And when the time drew near that Israel must die, he called his son Joseph and said to him, "If now I have found favour in your sight, put your hand under my thigh, and promise to deal loyally and truly with me. Do not bury me in Egypt, ³⁰but let me lie with my fathers; carry me out of Egypt and bury me in their burying place." He answered, "I will do as you have said." ³¹And he said, "Swear to me"; and he swore to him. Then Israel bowed himself upon the head of his bed.

No doubt Jacob had enjoyed peace, prosperity and honour at the end of his days in the land of Egypt; but there was a great desire in his heart that his own land should be his last resting-place.

It may seem unimportant where a man lies when he is dead; and so, in a sense, it is. When his spirit has gone to God it matters not where the worn-out tabernacle of his body lies. But, in the last analysis, there is something in man which defies our so-called common sense; there is the call of home. We may go to stay somewhere else in a far finer house than we possess; people may do everything to make us comfortable and happy; but in the end it is only in our own homes that we can be at rest and know real peace.

There is a lovely text in the *Psalms*: 'His soul shall dwell at ease' (*Psalm* 25:13). That means, 'His soul shall be at home.' We can only feel at home with ourselves when Christ has conquered the warring passions within us. We can only feel at home in the world when we realise that this is God's world and we cannot drift beyond his love and care. We can only feel at home with God when we learn that he is the God and Father of our Lord Jesus Christ. When that happens, wherever we are, life is at home, because life is with God.

A homely question: *what am I doing to make my home a lovelier and happier place?*

A FATHER'S VERDICT

Genesis 49:1-12

[1]Then Jacob called his sons, and said, "Gather yourselves together, that I may tell you what shall befall you in days to come.
[2]Assemble and hear, O sons of
 Jacob,
 and hearken to Israel your father.
[3] Reuben, you are my first-born,
 my might, and the first fruits of
 my strength,
 pre-eminent in pride and pre-
 eminent in power.
[4]Unstable as water, you shall not
 have pre-eminence
 because you went up to your
 father's bed;
 then you defiled it — you went
 up to my couch!
[5]Simeon and Levi are brothers;
 weapons of violence are their
 swords.
[6]O my soul, come not into their
 council;
 O my spirit, be not joined to
 their company;
 for in their anger they slay men,
 and in their wantonness they
 hamstring oxen.
[7] Cursed be their anger, for it is
 fierce;
 and their wrath, for it is cruel!
 I will divide them in Jacob
 and scatter them in Israel.
[8] Judah, your brothers shall praise
 you;
 your hand shall be on the neck
 of your enemies;
 your father's sons shall bow down
 before you.
[9]Judah is a lion's whelp;
 from the prey, my son, you have
 gone up.
 He stooped down, he couched as
 a lion,
 and as a lioness; who dares rouse
 him up?

A FATHER'S VERDICT (continued)

[10]The sceptre shall not depart from
   Judah,
      nor the ruler's staff from between
      his feet,
   until he comes to whom it belongs;
      and to him shall be the obedi-
      ence of the peoples.
[11]Binding his foal to the vine
   and his ass's colt to the choice
   vine,
      he washes his garments in wine
      and his vesture in the blood of
      grapes;
[12]his eyes shall be red with wine,
   and his teeth white with milk.

So Jacob came to the end of the road. He called his sons to him that he might give them forewarning of the things that should be. Reuben was unstable as water and would not excel. The man of compromise — and that is what Reuben was — can never attain to greatness. Simeon and Levi had in them a streak of cruelty. Had they not shown it with the others to their brother Joseph? For them too there was no greatness. But Judah, with all his faults, had ever tried to save life and not to destroy it. He had saved Joseph from death at the hands of his brothers; he had offered his life for Benjamin's life; and the honour is to be his.

And so indeed it was; for from the stock of Judah there came the Saviour of the world. Because he had sought to save and not to kill, because he was ready to lay down his life for his brother's sake, Judah was such that God could use him for his purposes. What greater honour could there be than that?

To think over: *do I train and discipline myself, that God may use me for his purposes?*

68

THE FRUITFUL BOUGH

Genesis 49:22-6

²²Joseph is a fruitful bough,
a fruitful bough by a spring;
his branches run over the wall.
²³The archers fiercely attacked him,
shot at him, and harassed him
sorely;
²⁴yet his bow remained unmoved,
his arms were made agile
by the hands of the Mighty One of
Jacob
(by the name of the Shepherd,
the Rock of Israel),
²⁵by the God of your father who
will help you,
by God Almighty who will bless
you
with blessings of heaven above,
blessings of the deep that couches
beneath,
blessings of the breasts and of
the womb.
²⁶The blessings of your father
are mighty beyond the blessings
of the eternal mountains,
the bounties of the everlasting
hills;
may they be on the head of Joseph,
and on the brow of him who was
separate from his brothers.

The old man's greatest song of praise was reserved for Joseph.
Observe what he says of him in verses 23 and 24. Joseph had suffered sorely from the slings and arrows of outrageous fortune; but
he had emerged unshaken and unbowed. Joseph had been tried
in the furnace of affliction but he had emerged purer and stronger
than ever.

Verses 24 and 25 stress the fact that the strength of Joseph was
the strength he gained from God. God never gave any man the
task of facing life alone. It may be that a man is bereft of earthly
help and support, but if he remains true there is ever the voice
whispering to him, 'I will never leave you nor forsake you.'

Joseph was indeed great, but all his greatness was of God.

A prayer: *O God, grant me a strength that is not my strength,
that I too in all things may be more than conqueror.*

BURY ME WITH MY FATHERS

Genesis 49:28-33

[28]All these are the twelve tribes of Israel; and this is what their father said to them as he blessed them, blessing each with the blessing suitable to him. [29]Then he charged them, and said to them, ''I am to be gathered to my people; bury me with my fathers in the cave that is in the field of Ephron the Hittite, [30]in the cave that is in the field at Mach-pe'lah, to the east of Mamre, in the land of Canaan, which Abraham bought with the field from Ephron the Hittite to possess as a burying place. [31]There they buried Abraham and Sarah his wife; there they buried Isaac and Rebekah his wife; and there I buried Leah — [32]the field and the cave that is in it were purchased from the Hittites.'' [33]When Jacob finished charging his sons, he drew up his feet into the bed, and breathed his last, and was gathered to his people.

Again Jacob expresses his last wish. It is to be buried with his fathers. There Abraham and Isaac lay. There he would lie too.

There is more here than the fact the Jacob wished to be buried in a certain plot of earth. He was conscious that he walked in a great succession and inherited a great tradition. What a priceless thing it is to be able to look back on our fathers, and to say, 'These were men of God; and I follow after them.'

Sometimes we strive to leave our children well equipped with this world's goods, and well furnished with this world's knowledge, when we leave this earth. But the best gift that we can bequeath to them is a name which was the name of a man of God, and a memory which will be at once a benediction and an inspiration.

For prayer: *let me thank God for godly parents and for the noble heritage into which I have entered. Let me determine before God to hand down to my children, and to those who come after, a memory which will inspire them.*

A FAITHFUL SON

Genesis 50:1-8

[1]Then Joseph fell on his father's face, and wept over him, and kissed him. [2]And Joseph commanded his servants the physicians to embalm his father. So the physicians embalmed Israel; [3]forty days were required for it, for so many are required for embalming. And the Egyptians wept for him seventy days.

[4]And when the days for weeping for him were past, Joseph spoke to the household of Pharaoh, saying, ''If now I have found favour in your eyes, speak, I pray you, in the ears of Pharaoh, saying, [5]My father made me swear, saying, 'I am about to die: in my tomb which I hewed out for myself in the land of Canaan, there shall you bury me.' Now therefore let me go up, I pray you, and bury my father; then I will return.'' [6]And Pharaoh answered, ''Go up, and bury your father, as he made you swear.'' [7]So Joseph went up to bury his father; and with him went up all the servants of Pharaoh, and the elders of his household, and all the elders of the land of Egypt, [8]as well as all the household of Joseph, and his brothers, and his father's household ... .

It might have been easy to regard Jacob's last wish as an old man's whim: and to find excuses not to carry it out. Joseph could have said that his responsibilities in Egypt made it impossible; that he had too much on his hands to go to perform the last duties to his father. But Joseph was the faithful son to the end.

When his mother died, Sir James Barrie wrote 'I can look back and I cannot see the smallest thing undone.' Blessed is the man who, looking back, can truly make that claim. The day comes inevitably when nothing hurts us so much as the things we failed to do and when nothing comforts us as much as the things we did. 'Honour your father and your mother,' says the commandment; there is joy for the man who can answer, 'This have I done.'

A prayer: *help me, O God, ever to love and honour the parents with whom you have blessed me: and if they are gone from me to you, help me to keep their memory fresh.*

GOD MEANT IT FOR GOOD

Genesis 50:15-21

[15]When Joseph's brothers saw that their father was dead, they said "It may be that Joseph will hate us and pay us back for all the evil which we did to him." [16]So they sent a message to Joseph, saying, "Your father gave this command before he died, [17]'Say to Joseph, Forgive, I pray you, the transgression of your brothers and their sin, because they did evil to you.' And now, we pray you, forgive the transgression of the servants of the God of your father." Joseph wept when they spoke to him. [18]His brothers also came and fell down before him, and said, "Behold we are your servants." [19]But Joseph said to them, "Fear not, for am I in the place of God? [20]As for you, you meant evil against me; but God meant it for good, to bring it about that many people should be kept alive, as they are today. [21]So do not fear; I will provide for you and your little ones." Thus he reassured them and comforted them.

Once again, at the end, the guilty conscience of Joseph's brothers troubled them. They feared that, with Jacob gone, Joseph might be rid of the restraint of love for his father, and might proceed to take a swift vengeance upon them. So they offered him the humblest submission.

Note Joseph's twofold answer. First, he asks, 'Am I in the place of God?' (v19). Joseph had learned that judgment belongs to God. He himself proposed to judge no man. Only God can judge the human heart and there Joseph was content to leave it; would not the Judge of all the earth do right?

Then he looks back over the years, with their disasters and triumphs, their sorrows and joys; and in the end he gives his verdict on life: 'You thought evil against me; but God meant it for good' (v20). There is a plan in the affairs of men; nothing moves with aimless feet. If we will only wait we shall see that the things we thought the greatest tragedies were the prelude to the greatest triumphs; that the prayers we thought unanswered received the richest answers of all.

We can be certain that in perfect wisdom, perfect love and perfect power, God is working for the best.

A text for the day: *'God meant it for good.'*

A prayer: *help me, O God, to trust you when I cannot see you: and to accept what I cannot understand, because I know you are love.*

THE BOOK OF JOSHUA

(Selected readings)

We now turn to *Joshua*. When the children of Israel reached the promised land after their long journey across the desert they did not find it empty. It had its inhabitants, people who had settled there for centuries. Naturally these people resented these newcomers from the desert and bitterly resisted their settlement in the land. *Joshua* tells the gallant story of how the Israelites gained a foothold under Joshua's leadership.

THE COURAGEOUS LEADER

Joshua 1:1-2, 5-7

[1]After the death of Moses the servant of the LORD, the LORD said to Joshua the son of Nun, Moses' minister, [2]"Moses my servant is dead; now therefore arise, go over this Jordan, you and all this people, into the land which I am giving to them, to the people of Israel. ... [5]No man shall be able to stand before you all the days of your life; as I was with Moses, so I will be with you; I will not fail you or forsake you. [6]Be strong and of good courage; for you shall cause this people to inherit the land which I swore to their fathers to give them. [7]Only be strong and very courageous, being careful to do according to all the law which Moses my servant commanded you; turn not from it to the right hand or to the left, that you may have good success wherever you go.

It was a great responsibility which fell upon Joshua. When Moses died Joshua had to take over the leadership at the most critical of times, when the people were struggling to gain a foothold in the promised land. In such circumstances God's voice came to Joshua telling him certain things.

(1) God spoke to him of the need for courage. All the world admires a brave man. When Danton, the great Frenchman, was being led to the guillotine to be executed, they heard him murmur to himself, "Danton, no weakness!'

To have courage is not the same as having no fear. Real courage is to be afraid to do a thing and yet to compel oneself to do it. Never be ashamed of being afraid; but always be ashamed of letting fear stop us from doing what we know is right.

(2) God spoke to him of the need for obedience. There could be no success or prosperity except by obedience to the commandments of God. As *Judges* shows, national sin was always followed by national misfortune.

(3) God spoke to him of the need to study God's word. The man who will not study God's word robs himself of the supreme guidance for the way of life. The traveller who refuses a map cannot complain if he ends in disaster.

(4) But God made to Joshua the greatest of promises. "I will not fail thee, nor forsake thee' (v5). Dangers might lie ahead but nothing could separate him from the presence of God. That promise holds good for us.

To rest my heart upon: *there is nothing that can separate me from the love of God in Christ Jesus my Lord.*

DUTY TO OTHERS

Joshua 1:10-15

[10]Then Joshua commanded the officers of the people, [11] "Pass through the camp, and command the people, 'Prepare your provisions; for within three days you are to pass over this Jordan, to go in to take possession of the land which the LORD your God gives you to possess.'"

[12]And to the Reubenites, the Gadites, and the half-tribe of Manas'seh Joshua said, [13]"Remember the word which Moses the servant of the LORD commanded you, saying, 'The LORD your God is providing you a place of rest, and will give you this land.' [14]Your wives, your little ones, and your cattle shall remain in the land which Moses gave you beyond the Jordan; but all the men of valour among you shall pass over armed before your brethren and shall help them, [15]until the LORD gives rest to your brethren as well as to you... .

In *Numbers* 32 we read how the Reubenites, the Gadites and half the tribe of Manasseh had settled on the east side of the Jordan. They were cattlemen and the land suited them there. Moses had allowed this on condition that when their help was needed they would ungrudgingly give it. Now the time for the struggle has come, Joshua reminds them of their promise and they do not hesitate to honour it.

We must never enjoy selfish pleasure while others still have not enough. It may be that life is easy for us; but it is hard for others, and we must not forget them. We must have such a sense of responsibility towards our fellow men that our consciences will not allow us to enjoy too much while others have too little. Our supreme example is our blessed Lord who had equality with God as his right but who gave it all up for our sakes (*Philippians* 2:5-11).

Questions to ponder: *how can we keep ourselves continually in the realisation that Jesus is not a figure in a book, about whom we read, but someone with whom we ought to live every day? What difference to our lives should this great thought of the risen and ever-present Lord make?*

AN UNLIKELY ALLY

Joshua 2:1-6

> [1]And Joshua the son of Nun sent two men secretly from Shittim as spies, saying, "Go, view the land, especially Jericho." And they went, and came into the house of a harlot whose name was Rahab, and lodged there. [2]And it was told the king of Jericho, "Behold, certain men of Israel have come here tonight to search out the land." [3]Then the king of Jericho sent to Rahab, saying, "Bring forth the men that have come to you, who entered your house; for they have come to search out all the land." [4]But the woman had taken the two men and hidden them; and she said, "True, men came to me, but I did not know where they came from; [5]and when the gate was to be closed, at dark, the men went out; where the men went I do not know; pursue them quickly, for you will overtake them." [6]But she had brought them up to the roof, and hid them with the stalks of flax which she had laid in order on the roof.

Jericho was one of the main obstacles in the way of the children of Israel; so Joshua sent out two spies to see how best it might be taken. These men went into the city and this chapter tells the adventurous story of how they would never have escaped with their lives had it not been for the help of Rahab. Rahab was a woman whose character was anything but good and yet she was used for God's purposes. Here is a lesson for us. (1) This shows us that we must never look with contempt on any person. It is so easy to be self-righteous and to draw away from someone whom we think beneath our level. (2) We must never despair of anyone. There is no one for whom we can say that the future is hopeless. The all-sufficient grace of God can take any life and change it and use it for his purposes. Rahab was the most unlikely of allies, yet she too has her place in the history of Israel.

A prayer: *keep me, O God, from being too critical and too censorious. Help me to judge not, that I be not judged.*

LEST WE FORGET

Joshua 4:4-7

> [4]Then Joshua called the twelve men from the people of Israel, whom he had appointed, a man from each tribe; [5]and Joshua said to them, ''Pass on before the ark of the LORD your God into the midst of the Jordan, and take up each of you a stone upon his shoulder, according to the number of the tribes of the people of Israel, [6]that this may be a sign among you, when your children ask in time to come, 'What do those stones mean to you?' [7]Then you shall tell them that the waters of the Jordan were cut off before the ark of the covenant of the LORD; when it passed over the Jordan, the waters of the Jordan were cut off. So these stones shall be to the people of Israel a memorial for ever.''

The children of Israel were wondrously helped in the crossing of the Jordan; Joshua had given orders that a man from each tribe should take a stone from the bed of the river and that with these stones a monument should be built. Then in the years to come when the children asked, 'What is the meaning of these stones?' the old story would be told again and the help of God's hand would be remembered.

It is so easy to forget. The Greeks talked of 'time which wipes all things out,' as if our memories were slates and time a sponge which wiped out the remembrance of the things we should remember.

We should remember our failures. Such memories will keep us humble and will teach us that we cannot walk alone.

We should remember our successes. Such memories will bring us roses in life's December and make us bless God for all his benefits.

We should remember what men have done for us. God save us from the sin of ingratitude.

Above all, we should remember what God has done for us.

A prayer: teach me, O God, to count my blessings. Help me to be sure that the hand which has guided the past will also guard the future.

MISFORTUNE FOLLOWS SIN

Joshua 7:1-5

¹But the people of Israel broke faith in regard to the devoted things; for Achan the son of Carmi, son of Zabdi, son of Zerah, of the tribe of Judah, took some of the devoted things; and the anger of the LORD burned against the people of Israel.

²Joshua sent men from Jericho to Ai, which is near Beth-aven, east of Bethel, and said to them, "Go up and spy out the land." And the men went up and spied out Ai. ³And they returned to Joshua, and said to him, "Let not all the people go up, but let about two or three thousand men go up and attack Ai; do not make the whole people toil up there, for they are but few." ⁴So about three thousand went up there from the people; and they fled before the men of Ai, ⁵and the men of Ai killed about thirty-six men of them, and chased them before the gate as far as Sheb'arim, and slew them at the descent. And the hearts of the people melted, and became as water.

The command of God was broken by Achan. The results were disastrous, for when the children of Israel proceeded against Ai, a little city which should have been easily overcome, they were completely defeated and routed. National misfortune always follows national sin.

J A Froude, after a lifetime spent in the study of history, gave it as his verdict, 'One lesson and only one history may be said to teach and to repeat with distinctness; that the world is built somehow on moral foundations; that in the long run it is well with the good and in the long run it is ill with the wicked.' Empire after empire has fallen when moral degeneration set in.

That could happen today. If a nation or an empire is to be great, it must be based on obedience to the law of God.

A prayer: *O God, teach me that there is no other way to true greatness than by serving you.*

ACTION!

Joshua 7:10-13

[10]The LORD said to Joshua, "Arise, why have you thus fallen upon your face? [11]Israel has sinned; they have transgressed my covenant which I commanded them; they have taken some of the devoted things; they have stolen, and lied, and put them among their own stuff. [12]Therefore the people of Israel cannot stand before their enemies; they turn their backs before their enemies, because they have become a thing for destruction. I will be with you no more, unless you destroy the devoted things from among you. [13]Up, sanctify the people, and say, 'Sanctify yourselves for tomorrow; for thus says the LORD, God of Israel, "There are devoted things in the midst of you, O Israel; you cannot stand before your enemies, until you take away the devoted things from among you.' ...'"

In his despair at what had happened Joshua prostrated himself before God. Look carefully at God's words to him. 'Get up; why have you thus fallen upon your face?' (v10). The whole passage insists that if something has gone wrong what is needed is action to put it right. Tears, regret and sorrow are not enough; the wrong thing must be dealt with.

In grim days of Scottish history Lord Rea and Lord Ramsay were talking. Lord Rea said to Lord Ramsay, 'Well, God mend all.' Ramsay replied, "Faith, Donald, we must help him to mend it." Idle regrets will get us nowhere. When things go wrong we must be up and doing in the strength of God.

A prayer: *O God, give me clear sight to see where things are wrong and give me grace and strength to mend them.*

THE WAY OF TEMPTATION

Joshua 7:16-21

16So Joshua arose early in the morning, and brought Israel near tribe by tribe, and the tribe of Judah was taken; 17and he brought near the families of Judah, and the family of the Zer'ahites was taken; and he brought near the family of the Zer'ahites man by man, and Zabdi was taken; 18and he brought near his household man by man, and Achan the son of Carmi, son of Zabdi, son of Zerah, of the tribe of Judah, was taken. 19Then Joshua said to Achan, "My son, give glory to the LORD God of Israel, and render praise to him; and tell me now what you have done; do not hide it from me." 20And Achan answered Joshua, "Of a truth I have sinned against the LORD God of Israel, and this is what I did: 21when I saw among the spoil a beautiful mantle from Shinar, and two hundred shekels of silver, and a bar of gold weighing fifty shekels, then I coveted them, and took them; and behold, they are hidden in the earth inside my tent, with the silver underneath."

It was discovered that Achan was the man responsible for the people's sin and misfortune, and he was punished. Very vividly Achan confesses his sin in verse 20, and in that verse there is the whole history of temptation and sin.

Achan saw the forbidden thing. How often we fall because we allow our eyes to linger on forbidden things. We are like a child left alone in the house with a warning not to touch something. The child goes and looks at the thing again and again. If we would avoid sin, we must look to Jesus.

Achan coveted the forbidden thing. It is only when the heart is cleansed from the wrong desire that we are safe from sin, and only he who searches the heart can, by his grace, effect the cleansing.

Achan took the forbidden thing. If a man lets his eyes rest on what is forbidden, if he allows the wrong desire to settle within his heart, the battle is lost and the way to sin is open.

Achan hid the forbidden thing. Immediately a man has sinned his one desire is to conceal the wrong thing that he has done. But there is no concealment from God.

To ask myself: *do I ever allow my eyes to linger on forbidden things? Do I ever cherish wrong desires within my heart? Is there any thing in my life I seek to hide from men or from God?*

AN ENEMY'S STRATAGEM

Joshua 9:3-8,15

> [3]But when the inhabitants of Gibeon heard what Joshua had done to Jericho and to Ai, [4]they on their part acted with cunning, and went and made ready provisions, and took worn-out sacks upon their asses, and wineskins, worn-out and torn and mended, [5]with worn-out patched sandals on their feet, and worn-out clothes; and all their provisions were dry and mouldy. [6]And they went to Joshua in the camp of Gilgal, and said to him and to the men of Israel, "We have come from a far country; so now make a covenant with us." [7]But the men of Israel said to the Hivites, "Perhaps you live among us; then how can we make a covenant with you?" [8]They said to Joshua, "We are your servants." And Joshua said to them, "Who are you? And where do you come from?" ... [15]And Joshua made peace with them, and made a covenant with them, to let them live; and the leaders of the congregation swore to them.

The people of Gibeon resorted to a clever trick to gain an alliance with Israel. They came as if they had done a long journey and deceived Israel into granting them a promise of peace.

Temptation always comes to us in disguise. It says to us, if you do this, or take this, it will make you happy and you will be content. Temptation makes sin look attractive. If sin was always ugly to look at, if temptation would obviously always end in bitterness, no one would fall for it. But temptation is an expert in disguising the wrong thing so that it looks like a good and pleasant thing. One thing will nearly always save us. If we take the long view of things, if we ask, not, how will this look today? but, how will this look weeks, months, years hence? it will often keep us from falling. We must learn to look on things as God looks on them.

A prayer: *O God, give me eyes that pierce through the disguises of temptation and see things as they are.*

A PROMISE IS HONOURED

Joshua 9:16-21

[16]At the end of three days after they had made a covenant with them, they heard that they were their neighbours, and that they dwelt among them. [17]And the people of Israel set out and reached their cities on the third day. Now their cities were Gibeon, Chephi'rah, Be-er'oth, and Kir'iath-je'arim. [18]But the people of Israel did not kill them, because the leaders of the congregation had sworn to them by the LORD, the God of Israel. Then all the congregation murmured against the leaders. [19]But all the leaders said to all the congregation, ''We have sworn to them by the LORD, the God of Israel, and now we may not touch them. [20]This we will do to them, and let them live, lest wrath be upon us, because of the oath which we swore to them.'' [21]And the leaders said to them, ''Let them live.'' So they became hewers of wood and drawers of water for all the congregation, as the leaders had said of them.

This is one of the great examples of honourable conduct in the Old Testament. It was by a trick that the Gibeonites had obtained a promise of safety; but Israel honoured that promise. 'We have sworn to them by the Lord God of Israel; now therefore we may not touch them' (v19).

Sometimes we make a promise and then we find it harder to keep it than we expected. Circumstances may change; the cost of keeping it may be unexpectedly hard. It may be easy to find an excuse to break it. The true man knows that once a promise is given that promise must be kept.

There is one virtue on which all life is built and that is the virtue of fidelity.

A prayer: *O Lord Jesus Christ, I have given my pledge that I will be true to you. Help me to keep that pledge under any circumstances, to the end, so that, being faithful until death, I may obtain the crown of life.*

CALEB'S GREAT CASE

Joshua 14:6-9, 13-14

⁶Then the people of Judah came to Joshua at Gilgal; and Caleb the son of Jephun'neh the Ken'izzite said to him, "You know what the LORD said to Moses the man of God in Ka'desh-bar'ne-a concerning you and me. ⁷I was forty years old when Moses the servant of the LORD sent me from Ka'desh-bar'ne-a to spy out the land; and I brought him word again as it was in my heart. ⁸But my brethren who went up with me made the heart of the people melt; yet I wholly followed the LORD my God. ⁹And Moses swore on that day, saying, 'Surely the land on which your foot has trodden shall be an inheritance for you and your children for ever, because you have wholly followed the LORD my God.' ...

¹³Then Joshua blessed him; and he gave Hebron to Caleb the son of Jephun'neh for an inheritance. ¹⁴So Hebron became the inheritance of Caleb the son of Jephun'neh the Ken'izzite to this day, because he wholly followed the LORD, the God of Israel.

Long ago when the children of Israel had come to the borders of the promised land, spies had been sent out to investigate it. All but two had come back with a despairing report. Caleb had been one of the two brave men (*Numbers* 13;14:1-10). Now again in this passage Caleb is proving himself a gallant soul. He is asking for his inheritance, not a part of the country into which he might settle at his ease, but a land which he can only gain by conquest. Caleb was never happy unless he had something difficult to do.

In the old times when the knights came to King Arthur they wanted difficult tasks to undertake. Only thus could they prove their manhood and their devotion to their king. If we are set in circumstances where it is hard to be a Christian we should regard that not as a matter for lamentation, but as a challenge and an opportunity to demonstrate our devotion to our Lord.

IF YOU WANT IT, EARN IT

Joshua 17:14-18

¹⁴And the tribe of Joseph spoke to Joshua, saying, "Why have you given me but one lot and one portion as an inheritance, although I am a numerous people, since hitherto the LORD has blessed me?" ¹⁵And Joshua said to them, "If you are a numerous people, go up to the forest, and there clear ground for yourselves in the land of the Per'izzites and the Reph'aim, since the hill country of E'phraim is too narrow for you." ¹⁶The tribe of Joseph said, "The hill country is not enough for us; yet all the Canaanites who dwell in the plain have chariots of iron, both those in Beth-she'an and its villages and those in the Valley of Jezreel." ¹⁷Then Joshua said to the house of Joseph, to E'phraim and Manas'seh, "You are a numerous people, and have great power; you shall not have one lot only, ¹⁸but the hill country shall be yours, for though it is a forest, you shall clear it and possess it to its farthest borders; for you shall drive out the Canaanites, though they have chariots of iron, and though they are strong."

The tribe of Joseph were not satisfied with the portion of land allotted to them. Joshua's answer was, 'If you want more land, go and take it. Go and drive out your enemies; clear the forests; make an inheritance for yourselves.' Too often we want things to fall into our hands with no trouble or effort at all on our part.

Life teaches us that a man can achieve and attain almost anything if he is willing to pay the price in toil and in adventure. 'Genius,' as someone has said, 'is an infinite capacity for taking pains.' And as someone else has said, 'Genius is ninety-nine per cent perspiration and one per cent inspiration.' If there is something on which we have set out hearts then we must toil for it. It is work which in the end makes dreams come true.

God will not do for us what we can well do for ourselves. But when we put out our utmost effort, then *God* comes in and we and God together can do the greatest things.

A prayer: *God, help me not only to dream, but to work to make my dreams come true.*

CITIES OF REFUGE

Joshua 20:1-6

¹Then the LORD said to Joshua, ²"Say to the people of Israel, 'Appoint the cities of refuge, of which I spoke to you through Moses, ³that the manslayer who kills any person without intent or unwittingly may flee there; they shall be for you a refuge from the avenger of blood. ⁴He shall flee to one of these cities and shall stand at the entrance of the gate of the city, and explain his case to the elders of that city; then they shall take him into the city, and give him a place, and he shall remain with them. ⁵And if the avenger of blood pursues him, they shall not give up the slayer into his hand; because he killed his neighbour unwittingly, having had no enmity against him in times past. ⁶And he shall remain in that city until he has stood before the congregation for judgment, until the death of him who is high priest at the time: then the slayer may go again to his own town and his own home, to the town from which he fled.' "

It is often said that the Old Testament is a hard book, filled with stern, unbending laws. But here is an example of the mercy of the laws of the Old Testament. It was true that if a murder had been committed the duty of vengeance fell on the next of kin of the victim. But here it is laid down that if an injury has been done, as it were, by accident or unwittingly, then he who has done it may find sanctuary in these cities of refuge.

All through the bible there runs a distinction — the distinction between that which a man does deliberately and that which he does unwittingly. On the cross it is Jesus' prayer for the soldiers who were nailing him to it, 'Father, forgive them; *for they know not what they do' (Luke* 23:34). But let us never take this as an excuse. *We* cannot claim ignorance; *we* cannot claim that we do not know. We who have known Christ have known the highest; dare we fall short of it?

A prayer: *O Lord, you know my hot passions and wayward heart; sometimes by my own impulses I am swept away. Save me from that, but, even more, save me from deliberately sinning, from taking the wrong way when I know I am taking it.*

REST AFTER TOIL

Joshua 22:1-6

[1]Then Joshua summoned the Reubenites, and the Gadites, and the half-tribe of Manas'seh, [2]and said to them, ''You have kept all that Moses the servant of the LORD commanded you,and have obeyed my voice in all that I have commanded you; [3]you have not forsaken your brethren these many days, down to this day, but have been careful to keep the charge of the LORD your God. [4]And now the LORD your God has given rest to your brethren, as he promised them; therefore turn and go to your home in the land where your possession lies, which Moses the servant of the LORD gave you on the other side of the Jordan. [5]Take good care to observe the commandment and the law which Moses the servant of the LORD commanded you, to love the LORD your God, and to walk in all his ways, and to keep his commandments, and to cleave to him, and to serve him with all your heart and with all your soul.'' [6]So Joshua blessed them, and sent them away; and they went to their homes.

We saw at the beginning of our study of *Joshua* how the Reubenites, and the Gadites and half the tribe of Manasseh had already settled on the far side of Jordan; how they had been allowed to do so only on condition that they would give aid to their brothers who had still their battle to fight; and how they had honoured that promise. Now, for the moment, the struggle is over and Joshua allows them to go back to their own land. For them rest has come after toil.

There are precious truths here.

(1) The only rest that is really sweet is the rest that follows toil. It is only by contrast with the effort that precedes it that relaxation satisfies.

(2) There is no satisfaction in all the world like the satisfaction of a task well done. The deepest of all joys is to be able to say, as our Master said, 'I have finished the work which you gave me to do'.

(3) These tribes had paid their debt and they could go home with an easy conscience and a quiet mind. We owe both to our fellow-men and to God a debt which only a life-time of loving devotion can pay.

Thought for the day: *I can only rest in peace after I have toiled with fidelity.*

A LITTLE HISTORY

Joshua 24:1-6,13

[1]Then Joshua gathered all the tribes of Israel to Shechem, and summoned the elders, the heads, the judges, and the officers of Israel; and they presented themselves before God. [2]And Joshua said to all the people, ''Thus says the LORD, the God of Israel, 'Your fathers lived of old beyond the Eu-phra'tes, Terah, the father of Abraham and of Nahor; and they served other gods. [3]Then I took your father Abraham from beyond the River and led him through all the land of Canaan, and made his offspring many. I gave him Isaac; [4]and to Isaac I gave Jacob and Esau. And I gave Esau the hill country of Se'ir to possess, but Jacob and his children went down to Egypt. [5]And I sent Moses and Aaron, and I plagued Egypt with what I did in the midst of it; and afterwards I brought you out. [6]Then I brought your fathers out of Egypt, and you came to the sea; and the Egyptians pursued your fathers with chariots and horsemen to the Red Sea. ... [13]I gave you a land on which you had not laboured, and cities which you had not built, and you dwell therein; you eat the fruit of vineyards and oliveyards which you did not plant.'

Oliver Cromwell, in laying down a programme of education for his son Richard, said, 'I would have him learn a little history.' Joshua, when he wished to fix the hearts of his people more firmly to God, reminded them of their history. He seems to say to them, 'If God has done all this for you, what will you do for God?' John Newton used to say that, whenever he felt his heart cold and dead, he used to take 'a walk up and down amidst his past life', and when he saw what God had done for him the love in his heart kindled to a flame again.

When we think of what God has done for us it should move us to three things. It should give us a new gratitude. It should give us a new love. It should give us a new loyalty.

A prayer: *O God, forgive me my ingratitude. Help me to recall the great things you have done for me.*

THE ETERNAL CHOICE

Joshua 24:14-16,19

¹⁴"Now therefore fear the LORD, and serve him in sincerity and in faithfulness; put away the gods which your fathers served beyond the River, and in Egypt, and serve the LORD. ¹⁵And if you be unwilling to serve the LORD, choose this day whom you will serve, whether the gods your fathers served in the region beyond the River, or the gods of the Amorites in whose land you dwell; but as for me and my house, we will serve the LORD.'

¹⁶Then the people answered, "Far be it from us that we should forsake the LORD, to serve other gods. ..."

¹⁹But Joshua said to the people, "You cannot serve the LORD; for he is a holy God; he is a jealous God; he will not forgive your transgressions or your sins... ."

At this moment Joshua is acting like a supremely great leader.

He puts before the people a definite choice. 'Choose you this day whom you will serve' (v15). In life there can, in the last analysis, be room only for one loyalty. There must be some day when we say to Jesus Christ, I take you as my Saviour, my Master and my Lord.

> To every man there openeth a high way and a low,
> And every man decideth the way his soul shall go.

But Joshua puts before the people that choice at its hardest (vv19-20). He warns them with uncompromising bluntness what they are doing if they make this choice. One of the mistakes we have made in modern times is to make Christianity too easy. We tend to tell people that it will make no great difference if they become members of Christ's church or work in his service. We give them the impression that all they have to do is to live a good moral and respectable life. We should win more for Christ if we were to set the Christian life at its highest and its hardest; for the human heart still kindles at the offer of a great task.

A prayer: *O God, help me to choose this day whom I will serve. Help me to choose aright and help me through all my days to be faithful to my choice.*

EZRA AND NEHEMIAH

(Selected readings)

To understand the Jews properly we must take a bird's eye view of their history. The greatest of all the kings was David. He was at his greatest about the year 1000 BC. He was succeeded by his son Solomon, who died about the year 950 BC. With the death of Solomon there came the great disaster of Jewish history: the kingdom was split in two, never to be united again. The cause of the trouble was that Rehoboam, Solomon's son, sought to play the tyrant with such force that a revolt took place. In consequence ten tribes separated under Jeroboam and took Samaria as their capital: two tribes remained with Rehoboam and had as their capital the city of Jerusalem. Jeroboam's kingdom came to be known as the Northern Kingdom and Rehoboam's as the Southern Kingdom. For more than two hundred years these two kingdoms continued side by side, but then further disasters came. The Assyrians invaded the Northern Kingdom and in 721 BC Samaria fell. The great majority of the inhabitants were taken away to Assyria and were not heard of again.

Assyria was conquered by Babylon, and Judah, the Southern Kingdom, found herself between the two rival world powers, Egypt and Babylon. Judah was like a bone between two hungry dogs. She might have escaped with at best a troubled peace, but, against the advice of the prophets, she began to play politics. Babylon invaded her and Jerusalem fell in 586 BC. Her citizens shared the fate of her northern brethren and they too were carried away to Babylon. But there was this vital difference. The northern Jews had vanished from history; the southern Jews, even in Babylon, remained unconquerably Jewish. (*Psalm* 137:5)

In 539 BC Babylon in turn lost her Empire to the Persians, and the Jews received permission to return to their own land.

Now we move to *circa* 444 BC. Nehemiah, the Persian king's cupbearer, was a Jew. He held a position in Babylon which was the most trusted in the kingdom, but he was haunted by the thought of ruined Jerusalem with its shattered walls. It was his one dream to go back and begin rebuilding his ancestral city. By the kindness of King Artaxerxes I that dream came true. Nehemiah tells of the difficulties he encountered and how he conquered them.

In our bible *Ezra* comes before *Nehemiah*, but some scholars are agreed that the historical order is the other way round. For years that practical warrior Nehemiah laboured at his building, and then in 398 BC there came another great adventurer for God to Jerusalem. His name was Ezra. He was a scribe and an expert in the law. Just as Nehemiah had rebuilt the shattered walls of the city, so Ezra rebuilt men into the knowledge of God and obedience to his law.

A KING RECOGNISES GOD

Ezra 1:1-3

> [1] In the first year of Cyrus king of Persia, that the word of the LORD by the mouth of Jeremiah might be accomplished, the LORD stirred up the spirit of Cyrus king of Persia so that he made a proclamation throughout all his kingdom and also put it in writing:
>
> [2] "Thus says Cyrus king of Persia: The LORD, the God of heaven, has given me all the kingdoms of the earth, and he has charged me to build him a house at Jerusalem, which is in Judah. [3] Whoever is among you of all his people, may his God be with him, and let him go up to Jerusalem, which is in Judah, and rebuild the house of the LORD, the God of Israel.

The first six chapters of *Ezra* really go back to a period almost one hundred years before the work of Ezra and Nehemiah began. It was in 538 BC that Cyrus the Persian conquered the empire of Babylon. One of his first acts was to order the rebuilding of the temple at Jerusalem.

Cyrus was a heathen and knew nothing of the true God, but here we see a man with an instinctive reverence for God. In his heart of hearts he felt that God had raised him to that eminence in which he sat. He was only groping after God but he felt that he must not forget God; and he felt that one of the best ways in which he could show that wistful respect he felt was to order the temple to be rebuilt. From this we see two things.

(1) Somehow or other God never leaves himself without a witness. There is a light that lights every man that comes into the world. In every age and in every generation God has been speaking to men.

(2) Sometimes God uses the most unlikely instruments for his service. Cyrus was a heathen Persian king, yet God used him. Over all the affairs of men there stands 'the unknown steersman' whom men call God; and often those who do not know it are instruments in his hand.

To think about: *do we sometimes forget the great truth that, no matter what things look like, God is in control?*

OF THEIR ABILITY

Ezra 2:64-70

[64]The whole assembly together was forty-two thousand three hundred and sixty, [65]besides their menservants and maidservants, of whom there were seven thousand three hundred and thirty-seven; and they had two hundred male and female singers. [66]Their horses were seven hundred and thirty-six, their mules were two hundred and forty-five, [67]their camels were four hundred and thirty-five, and their asses were six thousand seven hundred and twenty.

[68]Some of the heads of families, when they came to the house of the LORD which is in Jerusalem, made freewill offerings for the house of God, to erect it on its site; [69]according to their ability they gave to the treasury of the work sixty-one thousand darics of gold, five thousand minas of silver, and one hundred priests' garments.

[70]The priests, the Levites, and some of the people lived in Jerusalem and its vicinity; and the singers, the gatekeepers, and the temple servants lived in their towns, and all Israel in their towns.

To this invitation of Cyrus to return to the city there responded 42,360 Jews. As we shall see, they fared ill; but at least it can be said of them that they did their best. In verse 69 there is paid to them the finest of all compliments. They found Jerusalem a shattered and ruined city. They had to set to the task of rebuilding and in that task they gave after their ability. Each man offered freely what he had.

There are only two tests of a gift. First, was it offered freely? An extorted gift is no gift at all. Better not to give than give with a grudge in the heart. Second, how much did it *really* cost the giver? It may well be that in terms of sheer cost the gift of a sixpenny piece may be a greater thing than the gift of a thousand pounds. Giving does not become giving until it hurts. What things the church could do, what things Christ could do, if men would give after their ability!

For our meditation: *am I giving to men and to God after my ability? Or am I trying to give men and God that which costs me nothing?*

THE ANCESTRAL CUSTOMS

Ezra 3: 1-5

> [1]When the seventh month came, and the sons of Israel were in the towns, the people gathered as one man to Jerusalem. [2] Then arose Jeshua the son of Jo'zadak, with his fellow priests, and Zerub'babel the son of She-al'ti-el with his kinsmen, and they built the altar of the God of Israel, to offer burnt offerings upon it, as it is written in the law of Moses the man of God. [3]They set the altar in its place, for fear was upon them because of the peoples of the lands, and they offered burnt offerings upon it to the LORD, burnt offerings morning and evening. [4]And they kept the feast of booths, as it is written, and offered the daily burnt offerings by number according to the ordinance, as each day required, [5]and after that the continual burnt offerings, the offerings at the new moon and at all the appointed feasts of the LORD, and the offerings of every one who made a freewill offering to the LORD.

When this group of exiles returned to Jerusalem the first thing they did was to erect the altar and to make upon it the morning and evening burnt-offerings; they kept the feast of Tabernacles and all the ancient festivals of their fathers. In an entirely new and strange situation, in circumstances which were threatening and frightening, they found their comfort and strength in the old ancestral customs.

We may belittle custom and habit as we will, yet there still remains something fine in them.

(1) The old customs are clustered around with many memories. He is a dull soul who, when he sits at some ancient custom or enters some hallowed place, does not find himself surrounded by memories of the great things God has done for him and for his fathers who went before him.

(2) The old customs give us a sense of continuity. It is something to feel that we are doing something which has been done for generations. Especially is this so with the Lord's Supper. For over nineteen hundred years there has not been one single day when that sacrament has not been observed somewhere.

(3) The old customs give us a renewed sense of the unseen cloud of witnesses. They remind us that we are touching things, listening to things, sharing things which were precious to the saints and prophets of the past. We seem to touch hands with them.

LAUGHTER AND TEARS

Ezra 3:10-13

¹⁰And when the builders laid the foundation of the temple of the LORD, the priests in their vestments came forward with trumpets, and the Levites, the sons of Asaph, with cymbals, to praise to LORD, according to the directions of David king of Israel; ¹¹and they sang responsively, praising and giving thanks to the LORD,

"For he is good,
  for his steadfast love endures for
  ever toward Israel."

And all the people shouted with a great shout, when they praised the LORD, because the foundation of the house of the LORD was laid. ¹²But many of the priests and Levites and heads of fathers' houses, old men who had seen the first house, wept with a loud voice when they saw the foundations of this house being laid, though many shouted aloud for joy; ¹³so that the people could not distinguish the sound of the joyful shout from the sound of the people's weeping, for the people shouted with a great shout, and the sound was heard afar.

In due time the foundations of the renewed temple were laid. It was a great day but it was a day of mixed feelings. There were some who wept and some who shouted for joy so that the people could not discern the shout of joy from the noise of weeping.

Surely those who wept were those who looked back because they were old. They remembered the former splendours and thought of the years the locusts had eaten. Surely those who shouted for joy were those who looked forward because they were young. It was to the future that they stretched out eager hands.

Life is always like that. Let those who are old never disparage youth or think that all the fine things belong to the days beyond recall. Let those who are young never hurt those who are aged by belittling the contributions of the past to the present. The memories of age and the dreams of youth must walk hand in hand, for the church needs both its veterans and its new recruits.

Questions to ponder. *The people of the Northern Kingdom were absorbed by the alien peoples amongst whom they were taken to dwell; the people of the Southern Kingdom remained stubbornly Jews. How can we in our day and generation keep ourselves unwaveringly Christian in an unchristian world?*

THE REJECTED OFFER

Ezra 4:1-3

> ¹Now when the adversaries of Judah and Benjamin heard that the returned exiles were building a temple to the LORD, the God of Israel, ²they approached Zerub'babel and the heads of fathers' houses and said to them, "Let us build with you; for we worship your God as you do, and we have been sacrificing to him ever since the days of E'sar-had'don king of Assyria who brought us here." ³But Zerub'babel, Jeshua, and the rest of the heads of fathers' houses in Israel said to them, "You have nothing to do with us in building a house to our God; but we alone will build to the LORD, the God of Israel, as King Cyrus the king of Persia has commanded us."

In our introduction we saw how it was the custom for the victors in warfare to carry away the conquered to some strange and alien land. That had happened to the Jews and away in Babylon they had been utterly loyal to their faith and to their nation. But it was not possible to carry everyone away. Some had been left. Those who were left behind had intermarried with the strangers, who in their turn had been brought into Palestine.

Now the Jews valued racial purity more than anything else. Very recently if a Jewish boy or girl of a strict family married a Gentile his or her funeral was carried out. By intermarrying with the Gentile they had become as good as dead.

Those who offered help in the building were those who had intermarried and lost their racial purity. That is why their offer was contemptuously rejected.

We may think this rejection hard and unsympathetic, but it stands for the refusal to compromise with any tainted thing. No compromise! is ever a good Christian motto. Sometimes it is better to have no help than to accept help from the wrong people.

To think about: *are there any sources from which the Christian church cannot accept help?*

THE VOICE OF SLANDER

Ezra 4:6-8,24

> [6]And in the reign of Ahasu-e'rus, in the beginning of his reign, they wrote an accusation against the inhabitants of Judah and Jerusalem.
>
> [7]And in the days of Ar-ta-xerx'es, Bishlam and Mith'redath and Tab'eel and the rest of their associates wrote to Ar-ta-xerx'es king of Persia; the letter was written in Aramaic and translated. [8]Rehum the commander and Shim'shai the scribe wrote a letter against Jerusalem to Ar-ta-xerx'es the king... . [24]Then the work on the house of God which is in Jerusalem stopped; and it ceased until the second year of the reign of Darius king of Persia.

When the help of these people was rejected they resorted to slander. They wrote to the Persian king saying that these Jews had always been a rebellious and troublesome people and now they were rebuilding their city with a view to revolting against Persia. For a time this slander was effective; the king ordered the work to cease.

The evil man, if he cannot win by fair means, always resorts to foul means. Here is a test. If in order to achieve anything we have to resort to methods which cannot bear the full light of day, methods which our conscience tells us are not quite honest, then the thing we aim at is wrong. It is often the argument of the world that the end justifies the means. But the Christian must know that a thing which requires dishonest tactics to achieve it cannot be a good thing.

A prayer: *O God, searcher of the hearts of men, grant that all my deeds and words and even my inmost thoughts may be able to bear not only the full light of day, but also the scrutiny of your all-seeing eye.*

A WORK WHICH COULD NOT BE STOPPED

Ezra 5:1-5

> ¹Now the prophets, Hag'gai and Zechari'ah the son of Iddo, pro-
> phesied to the Jews who were in Judah and Jerusalem, in the name
> of the God of Israel who was over them. ² Then Zerub'babel the
> son of She-al'ti-el and Jeshua the son of Jo'zadak arose and began
> to rebuild the house of God which is in Jerusalem; and with them
> were the prophets of God, helping them.
>
> ³At the same time Tat'tenai the governor of the province
> Beyond the River and She'thar-boz'enai and their associates came
> to them and spoke to them thus, ''Who gave you a decree to build
> this house and to finish this structure?'' ⁴They also asked them
> this, ''What are the names of the men who are building this
> building?'' ⁵But the eye of their God was upon the elders of the
> Jews, and they did not stop them till a report should reach Darius
> and then answer be returned by letter concerning it.

For a time, due to this slander, the work of building was stopped.
But there were prophets who were men of courage and who bade
the people take it up again. Before these Jews there was a clear
choice. Whom were they to obey — God or men? What were they
to fear — the threats of men or disloyalty to God?

When we begin to do a great work there are two things which
may hinder us from bringing it to completion. The one is our own
innate laziness. In the first burst of enthusiasm we may fling
ourselves into the task; the routine, perhaps even drudgery, which
follows is a challenge to us. Let us pray for perseverance, one of
God's priceless gifts to men.

The other is the fear of men. As John Knox was being laid in
the grave, one who knew him well said, 'Here lies one who never
feared the face of man because he feared God so much.' H G Wells
once spoke of those to whom the voice of their neighbours sound-
ed louder than the voice of God. Long ago the Psalmist cried out,
'The Lord is my light and my salvation. *Whom* then shall I fear?'
If we love God enough we shall be delivered from all fear.

A prayer: *O God, my Father, grant me the gift of perseverance
so that when I begin a good work I may not lay it down
until I have completed it; and grant that at all times I may
fear nothing except to be false to you.*

THE APPEAL TO HISTORY

Ezra 5:6-8, 17

> ⁶The copy of the letter which Tat'tenai the governor of the province Beyond the River and She'thar-boz'enai and his associates the governors who were in the province Beyond the River sent to Darius the king; ⁷they sent him a report in which was written as follows: "To Darius the king, all peace. ⁸Be it known to the king that we went to the province of Judah, to the house of the great God. It is being built with huge stones, and timber is laid in the walls; this work goes on diligently and prospers in their hands. ... ¹⁷Therefore, if it seem good to the king, let search be made in the royal archives there in Babylon, to see whether a decree was issued by Cyrus the king for the rebuilding of this house of God in Jerusalem. And let the king send us his pleasure in this matter."

In the hour of their dilemma the Jews appealed to history, and history justified them, for when the Persian records were searched the decree authorising the building of the temple was found and the charge of the slanderers was branded as a lie.

We may learn: (1) The man with a clear conscience need fear no man. The Romans had a phrase in which they spoke of a mind conscious of its own rectitude. The man with a clear conscience can look the whole world in the face and tell it to do its worst.

(2) The best defence against slander is the truth. Once Plato was told that a certain man was spreading slanderous tales about him. His answer was, 'Then I must live in such a way that no one will believe him.' The truth will always shame the devil. That is not to say that the truth is always immediately victorious, but, as Conrad said, 'Justice holds the scales with an even and a scrupulous balance and in the end she will prevail.'

A prayer: *help me, O God, so to live and act that my conscience may be clear.*

THE WISE SCRIBE

Ezra 7:6-10

... Ezra went up from Babylonia. He was a scribe skilled in the law of Moses which the LORD the God of Israel had given; and the king granted him all that he asked, for the hand of the LORD his God was upon him.

7And there went up also to Jerusalem, in the seventh year of Ar-ta-xerx'es the king, some of the people of Israel, and some of the priests and Levites, the singers and gatekeepers, and the temple servants. 8And he came to Jerusalem in the fifth month, which was in the seventh year of the king; 9for on the first day of the first month he began to go up from Babylonia, and on the first day of the fifth month he came to Jerusalem, for the good hand of his God was upon him. 10For Ezra had set his heart to study the law of the LORD, and to do it, and to teach his statutes and ordinances in Israel.

The real bricks of which a city is composed are her inhabitants. It was important to rebuild the city of Jerusalem; it was still more important to rebuild the people into the knowledge of God. So from Babylon there came to Jerusalem Ezra the scribe whose duty it was to expound to men the law of God. Verse 10 gives us a summary of Ezra's way of life.

(1) He sought the law of the Lord. His one aim was to find the will of God. His one question was, Lord, what will you have me and this people to do? Happy is the nation whose leaders seek God's will both for themselves and for their country.

(2) It was Ezra's aim not only to know the law of God but also *to do it*. Many a man knows what is right and yet does what is wrong. Many a man tries to teach others to do what he has never done himself. Someone said of a Roman writer who wrote the finest books and lived the most questionable of lives, 'He says the finest things if only he had the right to say them.' To have knowledge of the truth and to act on that knowledge is the perfect way.

(3) It was Ezra's aim to teach God's statutes to others. No man who knows God's word can keep it to himself. We teach Christianity to others by showing them a Christian life.

For self-examination: *let me measure my life by the standard of Ezra's. Do I always seek God's will? Do I commend the Christian way of life to others not only by my words but also by my life?*

A PROBLEM OF PURITY

Ezra 9:5-9

⁵And at the evening sacrifice I rose from my fasting, with my garments and my mantle rent, and fell upon my knees and spread out my hands to the LORD my God, ⁶saying: "O my God, I am ashamed and blush to lift my face to thee, my God, for our iniquities have risen higher than our heads, and our guilt has mounted up to the heavens. ⁷From the days of our fathers to this day we have been in great guilt; and for our iniquities we, our kings, and our priests have been given into the hand of the kings of the lands, to the sword, to captivity, to plundering, and to utter shame, as at this day. ⁸But now for a brief moment favour has been shown by the LORD our God, to leave us a remnant, and to give us a secure hold within his holy place, that our God may brighten our eyes and grant us a little reviving in our bondage. ⁹For we are bondmen; yet our God has not forsaken us in our bondage, but has extended to us his steadfast love before the kings of Persia, to grant us some reviving to set up the house of our God, to repair its ruins, and to give us protection in Judea and Jerusalem.

Both Ezra and Nehemiah had to deal with one difficult practical problem. When the Jews were carried away to Babylon other peoples were brought into Palestine. But not all the Jews were taken. It is impossible to transport a whole nation. Both the Jews who had remained behind and those Jews who had come back, had contracted marriages with foreigners. Now to a Jew that was an exceedingly serious thing, for the Jewish nation more than any other stresses racial purity.

Ezra took the whole matter in prayer to God. He knew that if a man or a nation has done wrong there are only two things to do.

(1) The sin must be confessed to God. In our family and home life if we have been in error things are all wrong until we go and say that we are sorry. It is so with us and God for we are the family of which God is the Father.

(2) Strength and guidance must be sought from God to mend the matter. One thing is clear — no man by himself can conquer his own sin. We know from experience that that is impossible. But if we confess our sin we shall find God very kind; and if we seek his grace to conquer it we shall find that grace sufficient for all things.

A prayer: *O God, if I have done wrong, help me in penitence and shame to tell you about it. Grant then to me pardon and peace, and grant me the grace that alone can make and keep me clean.*

STERN MEASURES

Ezra 10:1-5

¹While Ezra prayed and made confession, weeping and casting himself down before the house of God, a very great assembly of men, women, and children, gathered to him out of Israel; for the people wept bitterly. ²And Shecani'ah the son of Jehi'el, of the sons of Elam, addressed Ezra: "We have broken faith with our God and have married foreign women from the peoples of the land, but even now there is hope for Israel in spite of this. ³Therefore let us make a covenant with our God to put away all these wives and their children, according to the counsel of my lord and of those who tremble at the commandment of our God; and let it be done according to the law. ⁴Arise, for it is your task, and we are with you; be strong and do it." ⁵Then Ezra arose and made the leading priests and Levites and all Israel take oath that they would do as had been said. So they took the oath.

In the end Ezra took stern measures and all the foreign wives were put away. It may seem hard to us, but we must remember the situation of the Jews. They were a small nation; they were surrounded on all sides by foreign peoples with strange and often immoral religious forms of worship. The Jews had a task to fulfil for God and it was necessary that they should keep themselves pure and clean. Ezra worked on a principle which is still valid; that every taint of evil must be avoided.

A prayer: *take from my heart, O God, even the desire for any forbidden thing. Make me to love you with a perfect love and to hate sin with a perfect hatred.*

THE KING'S CUPBEARER

Nehemiah 1:1-4,11

¹The words of Nehemi'ah the son of Hacali'ah.

Now it happened in the month of Chislev, in the twentieth year, as I was in Susa the capital, ²that Hana'ni, one of my brethren, came with certain men out of Judah; and I asked them concerning the Jews that survived, who had escaped exile, and concerning Jerusalem. ³And they said to me, "The survivors there in the province who escaped exile are in great trouble and shame; the wall of Jerusalem is broken down, and its gates are destroyed by fire."

⁴When I heard these words I sat down and wept, and mourned for days; and I continued fasting and praying before the God of heaven. ... ¹¹ O Lord, let thy ear be attentive to the prayer of thy servant, and to the prayer of thy servants who delight to fear thy name; and give success to thy servant today, and grant him mercy in the sight of this man."

Now I was cupbearer to the king.

'I was the king's cupbearer.' Nehemiah was the most trusted man of the king's staff in the whole of Babylon. In ancient days a king's life was never safe. There were always those who wished for his death. Poison was one of the commonest of the plotter's methods. Therefore the king's cupbearer quite literally held the king's life in his hands. Nehemiah was a loyal servant and the most important of the king's ministers. In this chapter we have a character study of Nehemiah.

(1) He was a man to be trusted. No one could question his loyalty.

(2) He was a man who had risen in the world. An alien Jew had become the right-hand man of the king. A good man will rise from the ruck of men in any situation.

(3) Though he had risen to greatness, he was not too proud to remember his less fortunate brethren:

(4) Nehemiah was not too great to confess his sins. He acknowledged that the misfortunes of his people were due to their disloyalty to God.

A prayer: *O God make me so true that all men will trust me. Make me so humble that I shall never despise another man. Make me so penitent that I may know that I ever need to ask you forgiveness for my sins.*

NEHEMIAH'S REQUEST

Nehemiah 2:1-5, 8

[1]In the month of Nisan, in the twentieth year of King Ar-ta-xerx'es, when wine was before him, I took up the wine and gave it to the king. Now I had not been sad in his presence. [2]And the king said to me, "Why is your face sad, seeing you are not sick? This is nothing else but sadness of the heart." Then I was very much afraid. [3]I said to the king, "Let the king live for ever! Why should not my face be sad, when the city, the place of my fathers' sepulchres, lies waste, and its gates have been destroyed by fire?" [4]Then the king said to me, "For what do you make request?" So I prayed to the God of heaven. [5]And I said to the king, "If it pleases the king, and if your servant has found favour in your sight, that you send me to Judah, to the city of my fathers' sepulchres, that I may rebuild it." [8]... And the king granted me what I asked, for the good hand of my God was upon me.

The news which filtered through from Jerusalem to Babylon across so many miles was bad, and Nehemiah was haunted by the thought of the trials and sufferings of his countrymen. One day Nehemiah's sorrow showed in his face. The king asked what troubled him; nervously Nehemiah requested that he might go to Jerusalem to help his people; and the king most graciously agreed.

Here again we see the qualities in Nehemiah's soul.

(1) He was a man of sympathy. His heart bled for the misfortunes of his fellow countrymen. Nor was his a sympathy which could be easily banished from his mind. It was said of a great missionary that he was haunted night and day by the thought of those who had never heard of Jesus Christ. And William Morris, it has been said, never met a drunken man upon the street without a sense of personal responsibility. The true Christian can never rid himself of a deep sympathy for his less fortunate fellow men.

(2) He was a man of courage. A Persian king was an oriental despot, and in his request Nehemiah took his life in his hands.

(3) He was a man of fidelity. Unless Nehemiah had been faithful, his request would never have been granted.

A question: *I say that I love God: but do I love* my fellow men *in such a way that I am driven to help them?*

NEHEMIAH FACES HIS TASK

Nehemiah 2:11-13,16-18

[11]So I came to Jerusalem and was there three days. [12]Then I arose in the night, I and a few men with me; and I told no one what my God had put into my heart to do for Jerusalem. There was no beast with me but the beast on which I rode. [13]I went out by night by the Valley Gate to the Jackal's Well and to the Dung Gate, and I inspected the walls of Jerusalem which were broken down and its gates which had been destroyed by fire. ... [16]And the officials did not know where I had gone or what I was doing; and I had not yet told the Jews, the priests, the nobles, the officials, and the rest that were to do the work.

[17]Then I said to them, "You see the trouble we are in, how Jerusalem lies in ruins with its gates burned. Come, let us build the wall of Jerusalem, that we may no longer suffer disgrace." [18]And I told them of the hand of my God which had been upon me for good, and also of the words which the king had spoken to me. And they said, "Let us rise up and build." So they strengthened their hands for the good work.

So Nehemiah came to Jerusalem. After touring the ruined walls he summoned the people to the task of rebuilding. Here we see in Nehemiah the qualities of a great leader.

(1) He surveyed the situation. He counted the cost.

(2) He faced men with the challenge of the situation. It is told that at one of the darkest hours of the war Winston Churchill was presiding over a gathering of the leaders of the allies. France had capitulated; Britain stood alone. Churchill painted the situation in its bleakest colours. After he had finished there was a silence and there were some who in that moment would have given up. Then Churchill looked up and spoke one sentence. 'Gentlemen,' he said, 'I find it rather inspiring.' The Christian sees in difficulties not a defeat but a challenge.

Questions to ponder. *Is it possible to love God without loving our fellow men? What should the Christian attitude be and what action should the Christian take in regard to the troubles and sorrows and injustices of this world?*

EACH MAN DOING HIS BIT

Nehemiah 3:1-2,8,27-8

> [1]Then Eli'ashib the high priest rose up with his brethren the priests and they built the Sheep Gate. They consecrated it and set its doors; they consecrated it as far as the Tower of the Hundred, as far as the Tower of Hanan'el. [2]And next to him the men of Jericho built. And next to them Zaccur the son of Imri built. ... [8]Next to them Uz'ziel the son of Harhai'ah, goldsmiths, repaired. Next to him Hanani'ah, one of the perfumers, repaired; and they restored Jerusalem as far as the Broad Wall. ... [27]After him the Teko'ites repaired another section opposite the great projecting tower as far as the wall of Ophel.
>
> [28]Above the Horse Gate the priests repaired, each one opposite his own house.

The work on the ruined walls was apportioned. In verse 28 we find that everyone repaired the place over against his house. Each man cleared up the mess opposite his own door. That is the way to get things done. Sometimes in a street of houses there is a fall of snow. If each householder will clear the bit of the pavement opposite his own front door the pavement will all be clear. We must always begin at our own door.

(1) A man's first duty is to mend *himself*. If we would spend our strength in correcting our own faults instead of criticising the faults of others, this would be a better world.

(2) A man dare not neglect his family. There are people who are so full of good deeds, so busy with community service, even so taken up with church work, that they do not give their own families the care and attention they ought to have. *Our first duty is at our own door.*

A prayer: *O God, my Father, help me to do the task that lies to my hand. Save me from dreaming of distant things and neglecting the things on my own doorstep.*

MOCKERY AND THREATS

Nehemiah 4:1-3,6-9

> [1]Now when Sanbal'lat heard that we were building the wall, he was angry and greatly enraged, and he ridiculed the Jews. [2]And he said in the presence of his brethren and of the army of Samar'ia, "What are these feeble Jews doing? Will they restore things? Will they sacrifice? Will they finish up in a day? Will they revive the stones out of the heaps of rubbish, and burned ones at that?" [3] Tobi'ah the Ammonite was by him, and he said, "Yes, what they are building — if a fox goes up on it he will break down their stone wall!" ... [6]So we built the wall; and all the wall was joined together to half its height. For the people had a mind to work.
>
> [7]But when Sanbal'lat and Tobi'ah and the Arabs and the Ammonites and the Ash'dodites heard that the repairing of the walls of Jerusalem was going forward and that the breaches were beginning to be closed, they were very angry; [8]and they all plotted together to come and fight against Jerusalem and to cause confusion in it. [9]And we prayed to our God, and set a guard as a protection against them day and night.

There were those in the neighbouring territories who did not want to see Jerusalem rebuilt. It was a threat to their power and influence.

(1) They used mockery. They said that if a fox leant against the wall it would collapse (v3). Many times the Christian will have to endure being laughed at. Often the Christian will have to be prepared to be a fool for Christ's sake. There is nothing so hard to endure as mocking laughter.

(2) They used threats. They said they would come and destroy Nehemiah and his friends before they knew what was happening (v11). Over and over again the man who starts a worthwhile work has to face threats from those whose comfort or whose self-interest is threatened. Joan of Arc said of God, 'In his strength will I dare and dare and dare until I die.' The Christian's courage is rooted in God.

To think about: *are there times when I allow myself to be deflected from what I know is right either by the laughter of men or by the fear of the consequences?*

WORKING AND WATCHING

Nehemiah 4: 13-17

> [13]So in the lowest parts of the space behind the wall, in open places, I stationed the people according to their families, with their swords, their spears and their bows. [14]And I looked, and arose, and said to the nobles and to the officials and to the rest of the people, "Do not be afraid of them. Remember the Lord, who is great and terrible, and fight for your brethren, your sons, your daughters, your wives, and your homes."
>
> [15]When our enemies heard that it was known to us and that God had frustrated their plan, we all returned to the wall, each to his work. [16]From that day on, half of my servants worked on construction, and half held the spears, shields, bows, and coats of mail; and the leaders stood behind all the house of Judah, [17]who were building on the wall.

To meet these threats, Nehemiah took certain steps. First he set his people in battle array. When the enemy saw that Nehemiah and his men were not to be so easily daunted they delayed their attack. Then Nehemiah resumed the work, but now each person worked with a tool in one hand and a weapon in the other; and half the people held themselves in readiness to rush with help wherever it might be needed.

Nehemiah set his people to work and to watch. In two senses we must ever be on the watch. We must be on the watch against temptation. We must be on the watch in prayer. It is when we wait upon God most earnestly that we can work most intensely.

Nehemiah kindled the hearts of his people by telling them that they were doing this work for the sake of two great causes (v14).

(1) They were doing it for God. Remember that God is seeking for those who will do his work. When he wants a deed done, he has to get a man to do it for him.

(2) They were doing it for their kith and kin. What we do affects our sons and daughters and future generations. If we are true to what is right the day will come when generations yet unborn will rise up and call us blessed.

A prayer: *O God, as I have entered into the labours of others, help me so to labour in my day and generation, that others will enjoy the fruits of the things I have done.*

NO EXPLOITATION

Nehemiah 5:1-7

[1]Now there arose a great outcry of the people and of their wives against their Jewish brethren. [2]For there were those who said, "With our sons and our daughters, we are many; let us get grain, that we may eat and keep alive." [3]There were also those who said, "We are mortgaging our fields, our vineyards, and our houses to get grain because of the famine." [4]And there were those who said, "We have borrowed money for the king's tax upon our fields and our vineyards. [5]Now our flesh is as the flesh of our brethren, our children are as their children; yet we are forcing our sons and our daughters to be slaves, and some of our daughters have already been enslaved; but it is not in our power to help it, for other men have our fields and our vineyards."

[6]I was very angry when I heard their outcry and these words. [7]I took counsel with myself, and I brought charges against the nobles and the officials.

Amidst all this work and activity there was one unhappy situation. Most of the returned exiles were very poor. And there were shortages. The city, so long occupied by a sparse population, found it difficult to provide for this new influx of returned exiles. As a result exploitation began. The few who possessed money lent it at high rates of interest or demanded the possessions of their fellow countrymen as security. Such a proceeding moved Nehemiah to wrath. He appealed to the sense of unity and to the better nature of the people and this evil was discontinued.

Nehemiah had a sense of community. He felt that he and his people were all in this business together and should share and share alike. The Christian can never be content to seek selfish ease and pleasure while others have not enough. He also had a burning passion for social justice. No nation can be erected on a basis of injustice. Nehemiah never lost sight of the individual man. He was eager to see that the humblest citizen was treated with justice and mercy.

To think about: *do I use all my possessions in the spirit of stewardship or in the spirit of selfishness? Do I realise that in the last analysis I do not own what I possess but that I owe it all to God?*

A GOOD EXAMPLE

Nehemiah 5:14-17

> [14]Moreover from the time that I was appointed to be their governor in the land of Judah, from the twentieth year to the thirty-second year of Ar-ta-xerx'es the king, twelve years, neither I nor my brethren ate the food allowance of the governor. [15]The former governors who were before me laid heavy burdens upon the people, and took from them food and wine, besides forty shekels of silver. Even their servants lorded it over the people. But I did not do so, because of the fear of God. [16]I also held to the work on this wall, and acquired no land; and all my servants were gathered there for the work. [17]Moreover there were at my table a hundred and fifty men, Jews and officials, besides those who came to us from the nations which were about us.

Nehemiah himself was a pattern of generosity. As the governor of the city he could have claimed as a right certain contributions for his own house and his own support. His predecessors had done it. Yet he kept an open table and exacted nothing from any man.

Nehemiah never demanded from others what he was not prepared to give himself. If he demanded that others should share, he himself shared.

If for the sake of the general good he demanded that others should abandon their chance to make money, he refused to use his own position for gain.

Perhaps the commonest of all sins — a sin of which we are all guilty in greater or in lesser degree — is the sin of demanding standards from others which we ourselves do not fulfil.

A prayer: *O God, my Father, who has given gifts to all men, and who never grudges the gift, give to me your own generous Spirit that I may find my happiness not in getting for myself but in giving to others.*

A SENSE OF VOCATION

Nehemiah 6:1-4

[1]Now when it was reported to Sanbal'lat and Tobi'ah and to Geshem the Arab and to the rest of our enemies that I had built the wall and that there was no breach left in it (although up to that time I had not set up the doors in the gates), [2]Sanbal'lat and Geshem sent to me, saying, "Come and let us meet together in one of the villages in the plain of Ono." But they intended to do me harm. [3]And I sent messengers to them, saying, "I am doing a great work and I cannot come down. Why should the work stop while I leave it and come down to you?" [4]And they sent to me four times in this way and I answered them in the same manner.

Sanballat and the other enemies of Nehemiah were not finished yet. Since mockery and threats had failed they invited Nehemiah to a conference. Their object was partly to make Nehemiah waste his time and so to hold up the work, and partly to get him, if possible, into their power to work him harm.

Read verse 3 and see Nehemiah's answer: 'I am doing a great work so that I cannot come down.' Nehemiah was a man with a sense of vocation. He had been given a task by God and in that task he had invested his life. Nothing must be allowed to hinder him. He refused to waste his time.

How many a man has become lost in by-ways and side issues, only to awaken too late to the fact that the essential thing is still undone and that it is too late to do it. First things must come first. One thing which no one can buy is time. 'Tomorrow' is the most dangerous word in the language. It is so easy to get involved in things which are not by any means bad but which are secondary. As someone has said, 'The second best is the worst enemy of the best.'

A prayer: *O God, give me clear sight and a sense of proportion that I may never be in any doubt as to which things matter most.*

THE COURAGE OF SELF-RESPECT

Nehemiah 6:5-11

⁵In the same way Sanbal'lat for the fifth time sent his servant to me with an open letter in his hand. ⁶In it was written, "It is reported among the nations, and Geshem also says it, that you and the Jews intend to rebel; that is why you are building the wall; and you wish to become their king, according to this report. ⁷And you have also set up prophets to proclaim concerning you in Jerusalem, 'There is a king in Judah.' And now it will be reported to the king according to these words. So now come, and let us take counsel together." ⁸Then I sent to him, saying, "No such things as you say have been done, for you are inventing them out of your own mind." ⁹For they all wanted to frighten us, thinking, "Their hands will drop from the work, and it will not be done." But now, O God, strengthen thou my hands.

¹⁰Now when I went into the house of Shemai'ah the son of Delai'ah, son of Mehet'abel, who was shut up, he said, "Let us meet together in the house of God, within the temple, and let us close the doors of the temple; for they are coming to kill you, at night they are coming to kill you." ¹¹But I said, "Should such a man as I flee? And what man such as I could go into the temple and live? I will not go in."

Still Sanballat and his friends pursued their policy of opposition. This time they charged Nehemiah with plotting rebellion and actually threatened his life. Then the false advisers, who had been corrupted by Sanballat, advised Nehemiah to take refuge in the temple. Nehemiah returned them one of the great answers of history. 'Should such a man as I flee?' (v11). Nehemiah was a man who valued self-respect.

In this world we have constantly to undergo two judgments. We have to undergo the judgment of our fellow men. In regard to them it is possible for us to put up a series of cloaks and disguises and so to hide the things that we wish no man to know. But we have also to undergo our own judgment, and we cannot get away from ourselves. Day in, day out, we have to live with ourselves. And if we cannot face self-judgment, then life becomes intolerable.

When we are tempted to do evil we must say, 'Can a man like me do this?' For if we fall into dishonour we are false to all the traditions, the heritage, the teaching that we have received. We bring grief to the hearts of those who love and trust us, and we spoil the future, for even if no one else knows what we have done we have lost our own self-respect.

A prayer: *O God, keep me straight and clean and true, that I may not break faith with those who made me what I am, that I may not bring anxiety and sorrow to those who love me, that I may not lose my own self-respect.*

THE PEOPLE ARE INSTRUCTED

Nehemiah 8:1-8

[1]And all the people gathered as one man into the square before the Water Gate; and they told Ezra the scribe to bring the book of the law of Moses which the LORD had given to Israel. [2]And Ezra the priest brought the law before the assembly, both men and women and all who could hear with understanding, on the first day of the seventh month. [3]And he read from it facing the square before the Water Gate from early morning until midday, in the presence of the men and the women and those who could understand; and the ears of all the people were attentive to the book of the law. ... [8]And they read from the book, from the law of God, clearly; and they gave the sense, so that the people understood the reading.

When Ezra arrived in Jerusalem he assembled the people and read the book of the law to them. Look at verse 8 and see Ezra's method of teaching.

He read distinctly. He did not deal with 'perhapses' and 'maybes'. He dealt with certainties, and left the people in no doubt as to what he meant. It is the duty of every Christian to think out his own faith and to be ready to give a clear account of it to any one who asks him.

He gave the sense of it. Too often we listen to words without asking ourselves, What does this mean? What does it mean for *me*? One of our difficulties in reading the bible is that we have heard its message so often that the words slip glibly over our heads and we do not grasp their meaning. Have you tried reading the bible as if you were reading it for the first time?

He caused the people to understand. Ezra was not satisfied until he felt that the people had really grasped his message. One of the great troubles today is that many of the critics of the church do not really know what the church is. Every one of us should be a propagandist for the church. A minister can only reach with his voice and presence comparatively few. In our generation the future of the church is largely in the hands of the laymen.

A prayer: *O God, help me to find the joy of bringing others to you.*

A question: *what can I do, what can my own church do, to ensure a strong, vigorous church in twenty years' time?*

THE LESSON OF HISTORY

Nehemiah 9:1-3,6-7

[1]Now on the twenty-fourth day of this month the people of Israel were assembled with fasting and in sackcloth, and with earth upon their heads. [2]And the Israelites separated themselves from all foreigners, and stood and confessed their sins and the iniquities of their fathers. [3]And they stood up in their place and read from the book of the law of the LORD their God for a fourth of the day; for another fourth of it they made confession and worshipped the LORD their God. ...

[6]And Ezra said: "Thou art the LORD, thou alone; thou hast made heaven, the heaven of heavens, with all their host, the earth and all that is on it, the seas and all that is in them; and thou preservest all of them; and the host of heaven worships thee. [7]Thou art the LORD, the God who didst choose Abram and bring him forth out of Ur of the Chaldeans and give him the name Abraham... .

This is a long chapter, difficult to divide up. At this moment the people of Jerusalem were re-dedicating themselves to God and were submitting themselves to his law. The leaders of the people gave them a bird's eye view of history to show them the guiding hand of God. From this three things emerge.

(1) All through history there runs the guiding hand of God. When we are in the middle of things or when we look at short sections of history, there may seem to be nothing but confusion; but if we take the long view we can see God's purpose. In our own day and generation let us put ourselves in line with that purpose of God and leave the ultimate issue to him.

(2) All through history there runs the disobedience of man. The lesson of history is that to spurn God's way is to invite disaster and ruin. No man and no nation ever disobeyed God and found true happiness.

(3) All through history there runs the mercy of God. If God had had the mind of a man he would have wiped out the world long ago. But God's patience bears with all our sinning and his love will not let us go.

A prayer: *O God, help me to see that all my freedom is in doing your will and my happiness in serving you.*

WALKING IN THE WAYS OF GOD

Nehemiah 10:28-9, 32-3, 39

> [28]The rest of the people, the priests, the Levites, the gatekeepers, the singers, the temple servants, and all who have separated themselves from the peoples of the lands to the law of God, their wives, their sons, their daughters, all who have knowledge and understanding, [29]join with their brethren, their nobles, and enter into a curse and an oath to walk in God's law which was given by Moses the servant of God, and to observe and do all the commandments of the LORD our Lord and his ordinances and his statutes. ... [32]We also lay upon ourselves the obligation to charge ourselves yearly with the third part of a shekel for the service of the house of our God: [33] for the showbread, the continual cereal offering, the continual burnt offering, the sabbaths, the new moons, the appointed feasts, the holy things, and the sin offerings to make atonement for Israel, and for all the work of the house of our God. ... [39]We will not neglect the house of our God.

The lesson of this passage is that religion brings not only privileges, but also obligations. Note that from verse 32 onwards the passage deals with the obligations and the responsibilities of the people to the temple and to the worship of God. We do well to ask ourselves, What are *our* obligations to *our* church and to its worship?

We must give our church our presence. How easy it is to find excuses for not attending divine worship. Unless sickness or unavoidable duty makes it impossible for us to be there, we must regard church attendance as a priority engagement.

We must give to the church of our substance. If the work of the church is to go on the costs of it must be met. Let a man examine himself and see how much he spends on his own pleasure and how much he gives to his church.

We must give the church our prayers. Many a preacher will bear glad and willing testimony that Sunday by Sunday his hands are upheld by his praying people. 'More things are wrought by prayer than this world dreams of.'

Thought for today: *do I give of my presence, of my substance, of my prayers, to my church as I ought?*

THE DEDICATION OF WORK

Nehemiah 12:27-8, 31, 42-3

²⁷And at the dedication of the wall of Jerusalem they sought the Levites in all their places, to bring them to Jerusalem to celebrate the dedication with gladness, with thanksgivings and with singing, with cymbals, harps and lyres. ²⁸And the sons of the singers gathered together from the circuit round Jerusalem and from the villages of the Netoph'athites... .

³¹Then I brought up the princes of Judah upon the wall, and appointed two great companies which gave thanks and went in procession. ... ⁴² And the singers sang with Jezrahi'ah as their leader. ⁴³And they offered great sacrifices that day and rejoiced, for God had made them rejoice with great joy; the women and children also rejoiced. And the joy of Jerusalem was heard afar off.

When the wall was finished it was dedicated to God with thanksgiving and praise. One of the best tests of any bit of work is, could I offer this to God? If work is so badly done that we dare not offer it to God then we have cause for shame. The Christian must ever be a workman who is not ashamed of his work.

Verse 43 will tell us certain things about Nehemiah's dedication. It was a day of rejoicing. There is no joy like the joy of work well done. Rest is only sweet when toil has been honest.

It was a day of sacrifice. When a great joy comes to us surely it must ever fill us with that gratitude which makes it absolutely necessary for us to bring a thank-offering to God.

It was a family occasion. The wives and the children rejoiced. The best worship of all is the family pew where young and old alike share in the worship of God.

It was really public worship. Every time we enter the church door we demonstrate publicly to others where our loyalty lies.

A prayer: *O God, my Father, grant that I may never fail in loyalty to your house.*

MAKING PROFIT OF GOD'S HOUSE

Nehemiah 13:4-7, 10-11

[4]... Eli'ashib the priest, who was appointed over the chambers of the house of our God, and who was connected with Tobi'ah, [5]prepared for Tobi'ah a large chamber where they had previously put the cereal offering, the frankincense, the vessels, and the tithes of grain, wine, and oil, which were given by commandment to the Levites, singers, and gatekeepers, and the contributions for the priests. [6]While this was taking place I was not in Jerusalem, for in the thirty-second year of Ar-ta-xerx'es king of Babylon I went to the king. And after some time I asked leave of the king [7]and came to Jerusalem, and I then discovered the evil that Eli'ashib had done for Tobi'ah, preparing for him a chamber in the courts of the house of God. ...

[10]I also found out that the portions of the Levites had not been given to them; so that the Levites and the singers, who did the work, had fled each to his field. [11]So I remonstrated with the officials and said, "Why is the house of God forsaken?"

There was a time when Nehemiah was absent from Jerusalem because he had to report back to Artaxerxes, his royal master. During that time Eliashib the priest was guilty of grave misconduct. He himself had appropriated the things that should have been given to the house of God. He had withheld the portion the Levites should have received and the Levites had had to till the ground for a living instead of serving in the temple services. Eliashib goes down to history as a man who made profit out of his church.

This may seem an ancient, irrelevant story. But it demands that we should answer one question: why are we in the church? Is it for what we can get out of the church, or for what we can put into it? There are those who use the church as a guarantee of respectability. Some never remember the church until they need its services for a funeral, wedding or baptism. But there are those — thank God for them — whose one desire is to serve and to give. And remember that in the end it is only those who give who truly receive.

Meditate upon this: *Nehemiah demanded, why is the house of God forsaken? (v11). Do I ever neglect the house of God?*

REMEMBER THE SABBATH DAY

Nehemiah 13:15-18

¹⁵In those days I saw in Judah men treading wine presses on the sabbath, and bringing in heaps of grain and loading them on asses; and also wine, grapes, figs, and all kinds of burdens, which they brought into Jerusalem on the sabbath day; and I warned them on the day when they sold food. ¹⁶Men of Tyre also, who lived in the city, brought in fish and all kinds of wares and sold them on the sabbath to the people of Judah, and in Jerusalem. ¹⁷Then I remonstrated with the nobles of Judah and said to them, ''What is this evil thing which you are doing, profaning the sabbath day? ¹⁸Did not your fathers act in this way, and did not our God bring all this evil on us and on this city? Yet you bring more wrath upon Israel by profaning the sabbath.''

Another abuse that had developed in Nehemiah's absence was the desecration of the Sabbath. It had become a day when men worked as on a week day; they bought and sold as usual. Nehemiah at once took steps to make men honour God's day. If ever there was a man of action Nehemiah was such a man, and it is therefore significant that he insisted on the observance of the Sabbath day. It is the simple truth that men cannot do without it.

They need it for physical reasons. Men need one day of rest. In the days of the French Revolution the authorities abolished Sunday. They found that they were compelled to reintroduce it because the health of the nation suffered so much from the lack of a day of rest. One of the characteristics of the time in which we live is the amount of nervous trouble and the number of nervous breakdowns. There can be little doubt that an important cause of that is that men have neglected God's day of rest.

We need it for spiritual reasons. It is true that all days are God's days, but unless we set apart one day each week when we give the foremost place in our minds and hearts to the things of God, we shall be in danger of forgetting God altogether. If we lose God's day, we shall take the way to disaster.

For meditation: *think of reasons for the decline in church going and for the increasing tendency to neglect the Lord's Day. What can we do to regain for the church and for the Christian Sunday their rightful place in the life of the nation?*

NEHEMIAH CLEANSES HIS PEOPLE

Nehemiah 13:23-6

²³In those days also I saw the Jews who had married women of Ashdod, Ammon, and Moab; ²⁴and half of their children spoke the language of Ashdod, and they could not speak the language of Judah, but the language of each people. ²⁵And I contended with them and cursed them and beat some of them and pulled out their hair; and I made them take oath in the name of God, saying, "You shall not give your daughters to their sons, or take their daughters for your sons or for yourselves. ²⁶ Did not Solomon king of Israel sin on account of such women? Among the many nations there was no king like him, and he was beloved by his God, and God made him king over all Israel; nevertheless foreign women made even him to sin.

Here we see Nehemiah dealing with a similar problem. Nehemiah, like a statesman, appeals to history. Was not Solomon a great king, and yet was it not his foreign alliances and his marriages with foreign princesses which sowed the seeds of Israel's degeneration?

We need look no further for a warning on this than to the fate of the other ten tribes. They were, as we saw, taken off to Assyria. There they intermingled with their captors and vanished from history. Nehemiah was convinced that if the Jews were to fulfil the destiny God had for them they must have no contact with any other faith.

Long years ago, Plutarch, the great Greek, heathen though he was, laid it down that a marriage between two people of different religions has little prospect of being a happy marriage. Unless two people can worship together there is something essential missing from their lives.

To think about: *let me examine my friendships and the company I keep. Is there anything in them which would make me think less of God?*

THE HYMNS OF ISRAEL

(Selected readings in the book of Psalms)

Of all books of devotion none has so nourished and comforted the hearts of men as the *Psalms*. Each psalm is a poem; and poetry speaks the language of the heart

But the psalms are more than poetry; in a way it may be said that the *Psalms* was the hymnbook of the temple in Jerusalem. In the second temple, every day had its own psalm. For instance, *Psalm* 92 was the psalm for the Sabbath day; *Psalm* 24 was the psalm for the first day of the week; *Psalm* 48 for the second day; *Psalm* 94 for the fourth day; *Psalm* 81 for the fifth day; and *Psalm* 93 for the sixth day.

As we read these psalms we are transported back to the fellowship of God's worshipping people, and we share in the hopes and fears, the longings and prayers, of Israel. Outward circumstances may change, but the human heart remains the same. The *Psalms* speak to us today as they spoke to men and women more than two thousand years ago.

THE HEART'S DELIGHT

Psalm 1

¹Blessed is the man
>who walks not in the counsel of
>>the wicked,
>nor stands in the way of sinners,
>>nor sits in the seat of scoffers;
²but his delight is in the law of the
>LORD,
>>and on his law he meditates day
>>and night.
³He is like a tree
>planted by streams of water,
>>that yields its fruit in its season,
>>and its leaf does not wither.
In all that he does, he prospers.

⁴The wicked are not so,
>but are like chaff which the wind
>>drives away.
⁵Therefore the wicked will not stand
>in the judgment,
>>nor sinners in the congregation
>>of the righteous;
⁶for the LORD knows the way of the
>righteous,
>>but the way of the wicked will
>>perish.

To the man who wrote this psalm, the law of God was a delight. He did not find it a dreary, burdensome thing that was a pain and penalty to keep. He found the law something from which he drew his strength as a tree on a river bank draws sustenance from the water.

He was a man of confidence. He was certain in his heart of hearts that in the end it was better to be faithful than unfaithful, better to be loyal than disloyal, better to be obedient than rebellious, better to be good than to be evil. He was sure that in the end the only happiness was in goodness and that wickedness brought its own penalty and its own punishment. It is true that the only way to happiness is the way of goodness, for through goodness we have fellowship with God.

A prayer: *O God, make me to know that I can only find my peace in doing your will. Bless me in all that I do and say. May each day bring me refreshment and opportunities for service.*

NO REMEMBRANCE OF YOU

Psalm 6:1-5

[1]O LORD, rebuke me not in thy
anger,
nor chasten me in thy wrath.
[2]Be gracious to me, O LORD, for I
am languishing;
O LORD, heal me, for my bones
are troubled.
[3]My soul also is sorely troubled.
But thou, O LORD — how long?

[4]Turn, O LORD, save my life;
deliver me for the sake of thy
steadfast love.
[5]For in death there is no remembrance of thee;
in Sheol who can give thee
praise?

Read again verse 5. See how the psalmist feels that death separates
him from God. Men in those far-off days had many things to learn.
They still had what we call a localised idea of God. They believed
that there were many gods and that each country had its own god.
They believed that each of these gods was real for that country and
that the power of a god was operative in one country, but not outside it. For them there was only one God — Yahweh. But they
had not yet risen to the thought of Yahweh as the God of all the
earth and the God of all the universe.

Think of this tremendous loyalty which made them cling to their
God even although they still felt that there were parts of the world
and parts of the universe in which his writ did not run. It was just
this utter loyalty which in God's good time led them on to greater
and larger truth. In *Psalm* 139 we find the greater truth most nobly
stated.

A prayer: *O God, help me to be very sure that in life and in
death I cannot drift beyond your love and care.*

THE WONDER OF MAN

Psalm 8: 1-4

¹O LORD, our LORD,
how majestic is thy name in all
the earth!
Thou whose glory above the heavens is chanted
²by the mouth of babes and inf-
ants,
thou hast founded a bulwark because of thy foes,
to still the enemy and the avenger.

³When I look at thy heavens, the
work of thy fingers,
the moon and the stars which
thou hast established;
⁴what is man that thou art mindful
of him,
and the son of man that thou
dost care for him?

The words 'upon Gittith' in the title of this psalm may refer either to some Gittite musical instrument, such as a harp, or to some Gittite melody.

The psalmist is impressed with the vastness of nature. He looks up and sees the limitless skies; he looks throughout the earth and sees its riches. Then he looks at man and sees him in all his littleness; he is struck with amazement that God has given all this greatness into the hands of man.

This, he seems to say, is God's doing and it is marvellous in our eyes.

Man's greatness depends on the fact that he can hold fellowship with God the creator. In the last analysis, he is kin not to the world but to God.

A prayer: *O God, help me to realise the greatness of my destiny. Help me to realise that, though man can control great forces of nature, he is helpless unless he himself is controlled by you.*

To remember specially: *'What is man, that you are mindful of him?' (v4). Dr Moffat translates it: 'And what is man, that Thou should'st think of him?'*

A LEAP OF FAITH

Psalm 16: 7-11

[7]I bless the LORD who gives me
counsel;
in the night also my heart in-
structs me.
[8]I keep the LORD always before me;
because he is at my right hand,
I shall not be moved.

[9]Therefore my heart is glad, and my
soul rejoices;
my body also dwells secure.
[10]For thou dost not give me up to
Sheol,
or let thy godly one see the Pit.

[11]Thou dost show me the path of
life;
in thy presence there is
fulness of joy,
in thy right hand are pleasures
for evermore.

The greatness of this psalm lies in the fact that it is one of the few
places in the Old Testament where a thinker rises to a sure belief
in personal immortality. The closing verses of this psalm are a leap
of faith. The writer had not by any deliberate process of thought
reached his conclusion. It simply seemed to him that all his days
he had known and loved God and that at the end of his days God
would not simply abandon him to annihilation. Think of the
character of God as we know it.

God is just. Can God then leave things in such a way that there
is one end for the righteous and for the wicked? Is all the struggle
for goodness to no point and purpose? Is all unrepentant sin to
find no punishment?

God is love. Can we believe that God created man simply to
obliterate him? Can we believe that there is no place where lives
which ended too soon will find their realisation; where lives which
suffered much will find their reward? The character of God as we
know it makes a life beyond the grave a certainty.

A prayer: *O God, help me, a child of time, to remember that
you have all eternity to work in. Help me to believe beyond
a doubt that I can trust your justice and your love.*

123

THE SHEPHERD PSALM

Psalm 23:1-6

¹The LORD is my shepherd, I
    shall not want;
²he makes me lie down in green
    pastures.
He leads me beside still waters;
³he restores my soul.
He leads me in paths of righteous-
    ness
  for his name's sake.

⁴Even though I walk through the
    valley of the shadow of death,
I fear no evil;
for thou art with me;
  thy rod and thy staff,
  they comfort me.

⁵Thou preparest a table before me
  in the presence of my enemies;
  thou anointest my head with oil,
  my cup overflows.
⁶Surely goodness and mercy shall
    follow me
  all the days of my life;
and I shall dwell in the house of
    the LORD
  for ever.

Here indeed the psalmist praises the love of God. As the shepherd leads the flock to the green grass and the water of the well, so God has cared for him and kept him.

Verse 4 should simply read 'The deep, dark valley'. Among the hills of Palestine there were narrow defiles among the limestone rocks, where robbers lurked and wild animals lay in wait. At such places the shepherd went first, so that the sheep following him might be safe. In every dark place of life God is in front of us to guide us; behind to guard us; above to protect us; and beside us to whisper his word to us.

Verse 5 speaks of an eastern custom. A fugitive, fleeing from an enemy, might come to an encampment. If, when he entered the tent door, the owner of the tent held out to him a pinch of salt and he tasted it, he was safe. That meant that he was the owner's guest and his enemy could not pass the threshold. God has made us his guests. If we accept God's hospitality the things that threaten us and the sins that pursue us can come no farther, for we are safe with God.

A question: *I have known this psalm all my life — but do I know the Shepherd as well as I know the psalm?*

124

THE ENTRY TO GOD'S PRESENCE

Psalm 24:1-5

¹The earth is the LORD's and
    the fulness thereof,
    the world and those who dwell
    therein;
²for he has founded it upon the seas,
    and established it upon the rivers.

³Who shall ascend the hill of the
    LORD?
    And who shall stand in his holy
    place?
⁴He who has clean hands and a pure
    heart,
    who does not lift up his soul to
    what is false,
    and does not swear deceitfully.
⁵ He will receive blessing from the
    LORD,
    and vindication from the God of
    his salvation.

This psalm falls into two parts which are intimately connected in thought. Verses 7-10 describe the triumphant entry of a king into his capital; but verses 1-6 describe the entry of the soul into the presence of God. The whole earth is God's and God's Spirit is everywhere, yet there are some places where the Spirit of God is specially present. But even there, even in the very house of God itself, we shall not meet God unless we bring something with us. He who would have fellowship with God to the fullest extent must have hands that have touched no evil thing; a heart which harbours no evil thought; a soul which has not gone in pursuit of empty things; a character which has been proved in its fidelity.

When we read that, it would seem to debar all of us from the presence of God. But we do not enter in our own merits, but in the merits of Jesus Christ. God does not only invite us to his presence; he clothes us with his grace in order that we may come.

Pray about this today: *read verses 3-5 again. Think how far short we fall of that: then think of the Saviour whose grace supplies our need.*

THE GRATEFUL HEART

Psalm 34:1-7

¹I will bless the LORD at all
    times;
      his praise shall continually be in
      my mouth.
²My soul makes its boast in the
    LORD;
      let the afflicted hear and be glad.
³O magnify the LORD with me,
      and let us exalt his name to-
      gether!

⁴I sought the LORD, and he answered
    me,
      and delivered me from all my
      fears.
⁵Look to him, and be radiant;
      so your faces shall never be
      ashamed.
⁶This poor man cried, and the LORD
      heard him,
      and saved him out of all his
      troubles.

⁷The angel of the LORD encamps
      around those who fear him, and
      delivers them.

Here a man lifts up his heart and voice to tell what God has done for him. He is saying, I know what God can do, for I have experienced his grace and power. But he wants others to share this sense of security and this sense of unseen resources around and about him. So in verse 11 he calls on others to take the way of obedience to God and then they too will share the happiness, joy and peace which are his.

This is a man who bears witness to the fact that all his safety and all his power are from God. He is a true man of God, for he has a great desire to share the secret with others. No man who has found God dare keep that preciousness to himself.

A challenge: *can I be a witness for God and a missionary for Jesus Christ today?*

LEAVE THINGS TO GOD

Psalm 37:1-7

[1]Fret not yourself because of
   the wicked,
     be not envious of wrongdoers!
[2]For they will soon fade like the
     grass,
     and wither like the green herb.

[3]Trust in the LORD, and do good;
     so you will dwell in the land, and
       enjoy security.
[4]Take delight in the LORD,
     and he will give you the desires
       of your heart.

[5]Commit your way to the LORD;
     trust in him, and he will act.
[6]He will bring forth your vindica-
       tion as the light,
     and your right as the noonday.

[7]Be still before the LORD, and wait
     patiently for him;
   fret not yourself over him who
     prospers in his way,
   over the man who carries out evil
     devices!

The psalmist deals with one of the most perplexing problems in the world. Why should it be that the wicked so often prosper and the good so often suffer misfortune? What are we to say to totally undeserved prosperity and totally undeserved suffering?

The psalmist does not offer a solution in logic; but he offers the only real solution. His advice is to leave the issue in the hands of God. He bids men to go on living in humble faith and in unswerving fidelity to God, leaving the matter in the hands of God, confident that in the end it will be well with the righteous and ill for the evil man.

In this matter we come back in the end to a very personal duty. That duty is not to envy, criticise or evaluate the lives of others, but to make our own lives as fine as we possibly can. The rest we may leave to God.

THE SOUL'S DEEP LONGING

Psalm 42:1-6

¹As a hart longs
for flowing streams,
so longs my soul
for thee, O God.
²My soul thirsts for God,
for the living God.
When shall I come and behold
the face of God?
³My tears have been my food
day and night,
while men say to me continually,
"Where is your God?"
⁴These things I remember,
as I pour out my soul:
how I went with the throng,
and led them in procession to
the house of God,
with glad shouts and songs of
thanksgiving,
a multitude keeping festival.
⁵Why are you cast down, O my soul,
and why are you disquieted with-
in me?
Hope in God; for I shall again
praise him,
my help ⁶and my God.

In its title this psalm is called a 'Maschil', which probably means 'a skilful psalm'. It had a specially delicate and beautiful musical accompaniment. The Chief Musician was the official who was in charge of the music of the temple services. This is probably one of the psalms that came from a collection called 'The Chief Musician's Book of Psalms.' The sons of Korah were a family of Levites; they may have had charge of the setting and arranging of the music.

The psalm is a cry of the heart. Once the writer was able to go up to the temple at Jerusalem, but now he cannot go. All he can do is to stand on the hill Mizar and gaze across the Jordan along the way that leads to Jerusalem.

For meditation today: *think of verse 1 at intervals today. Can you use it as a prayer, and sincerely mean it?*

A prayer: *O God, put in my heart a great longing for you. Open your hand and satisfy my longing with your fulness.*

GOD OUR DEFENCE

Psalm 46:1-7

¹God is our refuge and
strength,
a very present help in trouble.
²Therefore we will not fear though
the earth should change,
though the mountains shake in
the heart of the sea;
³though its waters roar and foam,
though the mountains tremble
with its tumult.

⁴There is a river whose streams make
glad the city of God,
the holy habitation of the Most
High.
⁵God is in the midst of her, she shall
not be moved;
God will help her right early.
⁶The nations rage, the kingdoms
totter;
he utters his voice, the earth
melts.
⁷The LORD of hosts is with us;
the God of Jacob is our
refuge.

This psalm celebrates one of the greatest deliverances in history. We may read about it in *II Kings* 18 and 19. The great Assyrian king Sennacherib had encamped round about Jerusalem and all seemed lost. Nothing could stand against his power. Urged to courage by Isaiah, the Jews refused to surrender. Then an amazing thing happened. One morning the army of Sennacherib had gone! The writer in *II Kings* 19:35-36 says that the angel of the Lord devastated the Assyrian host. Perhaps pestilence and plague suddenly swept through the army. Whatever happened, Jerusalem was miraculously delivered and this is the psalm of joy at that deliverance.

See how in verses 7 and 11 the refrain recurs. It is as if the psalmist said, our God is not an untried God; he has proved himself in history and what he has done he can do again.

Read carefully verse 10. *Be still and know that I am God.* We live a life of hurry and bustle; we must always be doing something or going somewhere. Shall we pause and listen in the stillness? If we do, we shall find God.

A prayer: *O God, help me always to put aside some part of the busy day to be still and to meet with you.*

THE TRUE SACRIFICE

Psalm 51:1-6

1Have mercy on me, O God,
        according to thy steadfast love;
    according to thy abundant mercy
        blot out my transgressions.
2Wash me thoroughly from my in-
        iquity,
    and cleanse me from my sin!

3For I know my transgressions,
    and my sin is ever before me.
4Against thee, thee only, have I
        sinned,
    and done that which is evil in
        thy sight,
    so that thou art justified in thy
        sentence
    and blameless in thy judgment.
5Behold, I was brought forth in in-
        iquity,
    and in sin did my mother con-
        ceive me.

6Behold, thou desirest truth in the
        inward being;
    therefore teach me wisdom in
        my secret heart.

This psalm is one of the highest expressions of real religion ever reached in the Old Testament. It is the cry of a man who in the very depths of his heart recognises his own sin. Remember that it is the good man who most deeply feels his own sin. Paul spoke of himself as 'the chief of sinners.' The nearer a man approaches to God the more he realises his own unworthiness. The psalmist, as he compares life with what it ought to be, is humbled by a sense of his own sin. But it is in the offering that he must make to God that he rises to his greatest height. Inevitably the idea had crept into Jewish religion that sin could be atoned for by some kind of sacrifice, and that if a man offered the right sacrifice to God he could, as it were, make his peace with God. With that the psalmist completely agrees; but the sacrifice which he knows a man must offer is not an animal upon the altar, but the sacrifice of a broken and contrite heart.

A prayer: *O God, help me to be truly sorry for my sin that I too may bring to you the sacrifice of a broken and contrite heart.*

HEAR MY CRY

Psalm 61:1-5

¹Hear my cry, O God,
    listen to my prayer;
²from the end of the earth I call to
    thee,
    when my heart is faint.

Lead thou me
    to the rock that is higher than I;
³for thou art my refuge,
    a strong tower against the enemy.

⁴Let me dwell in thy tent for ever!
    Oh to be safe under the shelter
      of thy wings!

⁵For thou, O God, hast heard my
    vows,
    thou hast given me the heritage
      of those who fear thy name.

The phrase 'upon Neginah' in the title of this psalm probably means that it was intended to be sung to an accompaniment of stringed instruments. There are three great ideas in it.

(1) It is a cry of present distress. The psalmist gives the picture of a man journeying along an exhausting road. What he needs is a great rock in whose shadow he can shelter either from the violence of the tempest or from the heat of the day. Life is a difficult way for him, and he prays God will be to him the rock of shelter which he needs.

(2) He remembers the past. Verse 3 tells how long before this he has experienced the help and strength which God can give. He is not praying to a God who is untried.

(3) In verses 4-8 he thinks of the future and once again he pledges himself to be faithful to God. His trouble is in the present; but he gains his confidence from past experience of God; and for the future he pledges himself to God.

A prayer: *O God, when I need you, help me to come remembering your past mercies and pledging myself to future service.*

To remember specially today: *'you have been a shelter for me'* *(v3).*

PRAISE WAITS FOR YOU

Psalm 65:5-9

[5]By dread deeds thou dost answer
us with deliverance,
O God of our salvation,
who art the hope of all the ends of
the earth,
and of the farthest seas;
[6]who by thy strength hast established the mountains,
being girded with might;
[7]who dost still the roaring of the
seas,
the roaring of their waves,
the tumult of the peoples;
[8]so that those who dwell at earth's
farthest bounds
are afraid at thy signs;
thou makest the outgoings of the
morning and the evening
to shout for joy.
[9]Thou visitest the earth and waterest
it,
thou greatly enrichest it;
the river of God is full of water;
thou providest their grain,
for so thou hast prepared it.

There are three thoughts in this psalm.

(1) Verses 5-8 speak of God's greatness in the events of history.
God bends circumstances to his will and shows his power in such
a way that all men must stand in awe of him.

(2) Verses 9-13 speak of the greatness of God in nature. The
things by which man lives are the gifts of God; without the providence of God man would die, for the very processes of nature
which give us food are in the hands of God.

(3) Yet it is to this God who is supreme in history, this God whose
greatness is seen in nature, that the prayers of men ascend. He
welcomes his children to his presence.

God is love *and* power. Power by itself might be a callous thing;
love by itself might be a helpless thing. But God's love is backed
by his power; and God's power is motivated by his love.

For meditation: *when I pray, do I remember the love and the
power of God? I cannot ask too much from God, if my asking is in accordance with his will.*

DEATH CANNOT SEVER

Psalm 73:1-3, 21-4

¹Truly God is good to the up-
    right,
    to those who are pure in heart.
²But as for me, my feet had almost
        stumbled,
    my steps had well nigh slipped.
³For I was envious of the arrogant,
    when I saw the prosperity of the
        wicked. ...

²¹When my soul was embittered,
    when I was pricked in heart,
²²I was stupid and ignorant,
    I was like a beast toward thee.
²³Nevertheless I am continually with
        thee;
    thou dost hold my right hand.
²⁴Thou dost guide me with thy
        counsel,
    and afterward thou wilt receive
        me to glory.

Verses 23-6 of this psalm are another great leap of faith. Behind these verses there lies a very great thought. It is the thought that an intimate relationship between a man and God entered into during life in this world cannot under any circumstances be broken. The thought is that if a man is in fellowship with God here and now there is nothing which can ever interrupt that fellowship. In such a thought death is not an end; it is scarcely even an interruption. It is merely a stage on the way.

So far from being the end of all things death is simply the beginning of things which are newer and more wonderful. When the famous minister, Dick Sheppard, died, a newspaper published a cartoon. It showed a bible lying on the bookboard of an empty pulpit and underneath the sentence, 'Here endeth the reading of the first lesson.' That is to say there was complete certainty that the second lesson was to follow. It is the same confidence as meets us so triumphantly in *Romans* 8:38,39, the certainty that nothing in life or in death can separate us from the love of God.

A prayer: *O God, help me to enter into such intimate fellowship with you that nothing in life or death may ever separate me from you.*

IN ALL GENERATIONS

Psalm 90:1-4, 11-12

¹LORD, thou hast been
  our dwelling place
in all generations.
²Before the mountains were brought
  forth,
  or ever thou hadst formed the
  earth and the world,
  from everlasting to everlasting
  thou art God.

³Thou turnest man back to the dust,
  and sayest, "Turn back, O children of men!"
⁴For a thousand years in thy sight
  are but as yesterday when it is
  past,
  or as a watch in the night. ...

¹¹Who considers the power of thy
  anger,
  and thy wrath according to the
  fear of thee?
¹²So teach us to number our days
  that we may get a heart of wisdom.

This psalm thinks of three things.

(1) The greatness of the eternal God. To God a thousand years are but as a watch in the night; before God the generations of men rise and pass away.

(2) The brevity of the life of man. At its longest man's life is but a moment. And many of us make our short and trouble-beset life far worse than it might be by our rebellion against God.

(3) The psalmist is certain that man's brief life can only attain to any kind of worth and peace when it is lived in obedience to and in communion with God. Man's dignity lies in the fact that he is a child of God.

This psalm is not an utterance of dark pessimism. It is a summons to lose man's little life in the fulness of the life of God.

A prayer: *O God, help me to rest my restlessness in your peace: to rest my weakness in your strength: to rest my little life in the vastness of your eternities.*

THE LORD OUR MAKER

Psalm 95:1-7

[1]O come, let us sing to the
    LORD;
    let us make a joyful noise to the
    rock of our salvation!
[2]Let us come into his presence with
    thanksgiving;
    let us make a joyful noise to him
    with songs of praise!
[3]For the LORD is a great God,
    and a great King above all gods.
[4]In his hand are the depths of the
    earth;
    the heights of the mountains are
    his also.
[5]The sea is his, for he made it;
    for his hands formed the dry
    land.

[6]O come, let us worship and bow
    down,
    let us kneel before the LORD, our
    Maker!
[7]For he is our God,
    and we are the people of his
    pasture,
    and the sheep of his hand.

This psalm is an invitation to worship God.

The psalmist calls upon men to worship God for two reasons.
(1) He is the creator and sustainer of all things. The earth, the hills,
the sea and the dry land are the work of his hands. He is supreme
in power. (2) But this God of might, majesty and power is not only creator of the world and of all men; he is the shepherd whose
sheep we are.

So here again the psalmist thinks of the power of God and the
love of God. We must bow ourselves before the power of God,
but we can rest ourselves in the love of God. An uplifting thought
is that all the vast power of God is moved by his love.

A prayer: *O God, help me to banish my fears by remembering
your great power and the wondrous love which opens the
resources of that power to me.*

Thought for the day: *'He is our God: and we are the people
of his pasture, and the sheep of his hand' (v7).*

GIVE THANKS TO HIM

Psalm 100

[1]Make a joyful noise to the
LORD, all the lands!
[2] Serve the LORD with gladness!
Come into his presence with
singing!

[3] Know that the LORD is God!
It is he that made us, and we are
his;
we are his people, and the sheep
of his pasture.

[4]Enter his gates with thanksgiving,
and his courts with praise!
Give thanks to him, bless his
name!

[5]For the LORD is good;
his steadfast love endures for
ever,
and his faithfulness to all generations.

This is one of the greatest of the psalms. For the most part, the
Jews believed God had little use for Gentiles. They believed that
they were the chosen people and that all other peoples were outside the mercy of God. But this psalm has the vision of nothing
less than a world for God.

We are reminded that all men are the sons of God and that the
heart of God will not be content until the last of them has come
home. There is therefore given to us the great privilege of making
glad the heart of God when by our prayers, our giving and our
service we spread the gospel throughout the world.

This psalm was — and still is — used at the daily service in the
synagogue. Do we always enter the gates of God's house with
thanksgiving and come into his courts with praise?

For prayer: *give thanks today for all who are taking God's good
news to people outside the church — both at home and in
far-off lands.*

THE GOODNESS OF GOD

Psalm 103:1-5

[1]Bless the LORD, O my soul;
    and all that is within me,
      bless his holy name!
[2]Bless the LORD, O my soul,
    and forget not all his benefits,
[3]who forgives all your iniquity,
    who heals all your diseases,
[4]who redeems your life from the Pit,
    who crowns you with steadfast
      love and mercy,
[5]who satisfies you with good as long
      as you live
    so that your youth is renewed like
      the eagle's.

These are the words of a man who stands and looks back across the years of life and who sees all of them bound together by the golden thread of the love of God. God has forgiven his sins and that is the first thing that all men need from God. God has healed his diseases. How many of us and how many of our dear ones has God brought back from the very gates of death! God has redeemed him from destruction. In this life we owe our safety to the providence of God and, in the next, we owe our confidence to his grace. God has crowned him with loving kindness and tender mercy. As he looks back, he sees that the things which looked like disasters and disappointments have been all in the wise providence of God. God has satisfied his mouth with good things. The day to day nourishment we receive, and the day to day strength that comes to us, are the gifts of God. When we think back upon our lives, we are dull and insensitive if gratitude is not awakened within our hearts.

    A thanksgiving: *for all your keeping, for all your grace, for all your love, for all your redemption, we praise you, O God of our salvation.*

THE MERCY OF GOD

Psalm 103:6-12

⁶The LORD works vindication
    and justice for all who are op-
      pressed.
⁷He made known his ways to Moses,
    his acts to the people of Israel.
⁸The LORD is merciful and gracious,
    slow to anger and abounding in
      steadfast love.
⁹He will not always chide,
    nor will he keep his anger for
      ever.
¹⁰He does not deal with us accord-
    ing to our sins,
    nor requite us according to our
      iniquities.
¹¹For as the heavens are high above
    the earth,
    so great is his steadfast love to-
      ward those who fear him;
¹²as far as the east is from the west,
    so far does he remove our trans-
      gressions from us.

Above all, the psalmist cannot but think of the mercy of God. If God had dealt with us as we deserve there could have been nothing but punishment. Only a mercy as wide as the universe itself could cover all our sins.

God's mercy comes from sympathy. He knows the feebleness and the frailty of man. How much more can we say that, when we remember that the Word became flesh and that God himself in Jesus Christ lived this very life, faced the very temptations that we face, bore the very pains and sorrows that we bear.

God's mercy comes from love. God is judge and king, but above all God is father; his feeling towards us is not that of a king looking down on his subjects but that of a father toward his children.

A prayer: *for the patience which bears with all my sinning; for the grace which is wide enough to cover every spot and stain; for the love which will not let me go: I this day thank you, O my God.*

A SONG OF PRAISE

Psalm 107:1-15

¹O give thanks to the LORD,
    for he is good;
    for his steadfast love endures
      for ever!
²Let the redeemed of the LORD say
    so,
    whom he has redeemed from
    trouble
³and gathered in from the lands,
    from the east and from the west,
    from the north and from the
      south. ...

¹⁰Some sat in darkness and in gloom,
    prisoners in affliction and in
      irons,
¹¹for they had rebelled against the
    words of God,
    and spurned the counsel of the
    Most High.
¹²Their hearts were bowed down with
    hard labour;
    they fell down, with none to
    help.
¹³Then they cried to the LORD in
    their trouble,
    and he delivered them from their
    distress;
¹⁴he brought them out of darkness
    and gloom,
    and broke their bonds asunder.
¹⁵Let them thank the LORD for his
    steadfast love... .

The refrain of this psalm is a summons to give thanks to God. It recurs in verses 8, 15, 21 and 31. Our sections fall into two parts.

(1) Verses 1-8. This is a great thanksgiving that God has brought his people back from exile. We too may echo this thanksgiving; for we were estranged from God and he brought us home to himself through Jesus Christ his Son.

(2) Verses 9-15. These verses are a song of thanksgiving for deliverance from prison and bondage. Nay, more, this bondage was brought on men by their own fault and their own rebellious disobedience; yet God in his mercy delivered them. Again we may echo this cry. We were in bondage to our sins, but, through Jesus Christ, God has wrought us a great deliverance and made us more than conquerors.

THE COMPLETE DELIVERANCE

Psalm 116: 1-7

¹I love the LORD, because he
    has heard
    my voice and my supplications.
²Because he inclined his ear to me,
    therefore I will call on him as
    long as I live.
³The snares of death encompassed
    me;
    the pangs of Sheol laid hold on
    me;
    I suffered distress and anguish.
⁴Then I called on the name of the
    LORD:
    "O LORD, I beseech thee, save
    my life!"
⁵Gracious is the LORD, and right-
    eous;
    our God is merciful.
⁶The LORD preserves the simple;
    when I was brought low, he saved
    me.
⁷Return, O my soul, to your rest;
    for the LORD has dealt bounti-
    fully with you.

Some grave peril had surrounded the psalmist and threatened his very life. Probably it was some serious illness. On his recovery, he lifts up his heart and voice in glad thanksgiving to God.

Verse 8 speaks of the threefold deliverance that God can work for those who put their trust in him.

(1) *You have delivered my soul from death*. Like other mortal men the Christian must die; but for him death is an adventure rather than a terror. It is, as someone calls it, 'a gate on the sky-line', leading not into unknown darkness but into the glory of the presence of God.

(2) *You have delivered my eyes from tears*. The Christian is not immune from sorrow; but his sorrow turns to trustful acceptance when he remembers that 'a father's hand will never cause his child a needless tear'.

(3) *You have delivered my feet from falling*. The pathway of life is as slippery for the Christian as for any man; the temptations he has to face are the temptations which are common to all. But he has within him grace which can keep him clean and which enables him to keep his garments unspotted from the world.

THIS IS THE DAY

Psalm 118: 20-25

[20]This is the gate of the LORD;
    the righteous shall enter through
        it.
[21]I thank thee that thou hast an-
        swered me
    and hast become my salvation.
[22]The stone which the builders re-
        jected
    has become the head of the corner.
[23]This is the LORD's doing;
    it is marvellous in our eyes.
[24]This is the day which the LORD has
        made;
    let us rejoice and be glad in it.
[25]Save us, we beseech thee, O LORD!
    O LORD, we beseech thee, give
    us success!

This is said to have been Martin Luther's favourite psalm. He said, 'Though the whole Psalter and all Holy Scripture is dear to me, as my only comfort in life, this Psalm has been of special service to me. It has helped me out of many great troubles, when neither emperor nor kings nor wise men nor saints could help.'

It is obviously a psalm written for a day when some great procession of triumphant thanksgiving to God was entering the gates of the temple.

For us there is one special and very lovely truth. 'This is the day which the Lord hath made', says the psalmist. 'We will rejoice and be glad in it.' The psalm does not say what day it was, so we may take it as referring, not to any special day, but to *every* day. It is not just on Sunday, but on every day of the week that, when we rise, we should say, 'This is the day that God has given me.' Every day is another gift from God and an opportunity to serve him.

THE LAW OF GOD

Psalm 119:33-40

³³Teach me, O LORD, the way of thy
    statutes;
    and I will keep it to the end.
³⁴Give me understanding, that I may
    keep thy law
    and observe it with my whole
    heart.
³⁵Lead me in the path of thy com-
    mandments,
    for I delight in it.
³⁶Incline my heart to thy testimonies,
    and not to gain!
³⁷Turn my eyes from looking at
    vanities;
    and give me life in thy ways.
³⁸Confirm to thy servant thy promise,
    which is for those who fear thee.
³⁹Turn away the reproach which I
    dread;
    for thy ordinances are good.
⁴⁰Behold, I long for thy precepts;
    in thy righteousness give me life!

This is the greatest of the alphabetical psalms. (See *Psalm 25*, above.)

The whole psalm glorifies the law which God has given to his people. The devout Jew did not look on God's law as a bondage or a chain, but as the greatest privilege he had. To study it was his delight; to keep it was his joy.

This section expresses the heart's desire of the psalmist that he might know and understand God's law; for only in keeping it was there safety, peace and joy. Truly, in doing God's will he found freedom and in obeying God's law he found peace.

A prayer: *O God, grant me the joy of obedience.*

SWEETER THAN HONEY

Psalm 119:97-104

[97]Oh, how I love thy law!
 It is my meditation all the day.
[98]Thy commandment makes me
  wiser than my enemies,
 for it is ever with me.
[99]I have more understanding than all
  my teachers,
 for thy testimonies are my meditation.
[100]I understand more than the aged,
 for I keep thy precepts.
[101]I hold back my feet from every
  evil way,
 in order to keep thy word.
[102]I do not turn aside from thy ordinances,
 for thou hast taught me.
[103]How sweet are thy words to my
  taste,
 sweeter than honey to my
  mouth!
[104]Through thy precepts I get understanding;
 therefore I hate every false way.

Here the psalmist remembers the great gifts that have come to him because he has dedicated his life to obey the law. He is wiser than his enemies, because he has discovered that it is always wiser to take the right way, even if it be the hard way. He is wiser than the ancients. He lives, as he sees it, in the blaze of God's fuller revelation. If he felt like that, how should we feel who have seen the glory of God in the face of Jesus Christ?

See how he stresses the fact that through God's law there has come to him wisdom and understanding. Other people are puzzled by the meaning of life and bewildered by its problems. But he who accepts the law of god has the way clear before him.

A prayer: *O God, make me wise, not in the things of this earth alone, but unto salvation.*

A LAMP TO MY FEET

Psalm 119:105-12

¹⁰⁵Thy word is a lamp to my feet
　　and a light to my path.
¹⁰⁶I have sworn an oath and con-
　　firmed it,
　　　to observe thy righteous ordi-
　　　nances.
¹⁰⁷I am sorely afflicted;
　　give me life, O LORD, according
　　　to thy word!
¹⁰⁸Accept my offerings of praise, O
　　LORD
　　and teach me thy ordinances.
¹⁰⁹I hold my life in my hand contin-
　　ually,
　　but I do not forget thy law.
¹¹⁰The wicked have laid a snare for
　　me,
　　　but I do not stray from thy pre-
　　　cepts.
¹¹¹Thy testimonies are my heritage
　　for ever;
　　yea, they are the joy of my heart.
¹¹²I incline my heart to perform thy
　　statutes
　　for ever, to the end.

It is said that Goethe the great poet and thinker died with the phrase upon his lips: 'Light! More light!' Life for him had been dark and death was a still darker mystery. But it is the glad witness of the psalmist that the law of God has lit the way for him and shown him what to do and where to go.

See how he insists that he has always been true. In verse 109 he tells how even when his life was in danger he kept the law; in verse 110 he says that even when his own enemies threatened him he kept the law; in verse 112 he insists that he will keep it *to the end*.

We cannot help thinking of the great New Testament counterpart of this. 'Blessed is he who endures *to the end*, for he shall be saved.' Our tragedy is that we give up too easily and too soon. It is those who are steadfast to the end who win the perfect joy.

For meditation: *have I a tendency to go my own way when Christ's way is hard? He bade me* take up a cross *and follow him.*

GOD THE PROTECTOR

Psalm 121

¹I lift up my eyes to the
    hills.
  From whence does my help
    come?
²My help comes from the LORD,
  who made heaven and earth.
³He will not let your foot be moved,
  he who keeps you will not
    slumber.
⁴Behold, he who keeps Israel
  will neither slumber nor sleep.
⁵The LORD is your keeper;
  the LORD is your shade
  on your right hand.
⁶The sun shall not smite you by day,
  nor the moon by night.
⁷The LORD will keep you from all
    evil;
  he will keep your life.
⁸The LORD will keep
  your going out and your coming
    in
  from this time forth and for
    evermore.

This is one of the 'Songs of degrees' which the pilgrims sang as they made the journey up to Jerusalem for the feasts. Very likely they sang this one as Mount Zion, on which the sacred city stood, emerged into view.

Probably 'hills' should begin a a new sentence (v1). Then the words 'From where comes my help,' would read as a question. It is not from the hills that the psalmist's help comes, but from the God who holds the mighty hills in the hollow of his hand.

This psalm says three things about the care of God. (1) It is unceasing. A man on guard may sometimes fall asleep; but the care of God never slumbers. Night and day God is watching over us. (2) It is a cleansing care. When we walk in the presence of God we are kept from all evil. How many things we would not do if we remembered that all life is lived in the presence of God! (3)It is a daily care. It is not a care that is confined to times of crisis. It keeps us in our going out and our coming in. As we sit in our homes, as we walk the streets, as we go about our daily work, the care of God is ever around us and about us.

A prayer: *give me a sense, O God, of your presence around me and about me, and your care encircling me, that I may feel safe.*

I WAS GLAD

Psalm 122: 1-2, 6-9

¹I was glad when they said
    to me,
    "Let us go to the house of the
    LORD!"
²Our feet have been standing
    within your gates, O Jerusalem! ...

⁶Pray for the peace of Jerusalem!
    "May they prosper who love you!"
⁷Peace be within your walls,
    and security within your towers!"
⁸For my brethren and companions'
    sake
    I will say "Peace be within you!"
⁹For the sake of the house of the
    LORD our God,
    I will seek your good.

This is another of the psalms which are called 'Songs of Degrees.'

It has three thoughts (1) There is the joy of the present moment when the sacred city came in sight. Is there always joy in our hearts as we enter the house of God? (2) There was the memory of the past. The history of David and his city passed through the pilgrim's mind. When we worship, something of the history of the Christian church and the memory of revered men and women who have worshipped in our own church in former years must be in our minds. (3) There was a prayer for the future. 'Peace' in Hebrew was not just the absence of trouble; it included everything that was for the good of a man, body and soul. So the pilgrim prayed for the good of the church in the days to come. When we enter God's house let us pray that we may be strengthened to play our part in the task of the church which lies ahead.

For ourselves: *when the Lord's Day comes, can we say that we are glad to go into the house of the Lord? Or is it only a burdensome duty to us? This psalm was written before Christ came, yet it can teach us much.*

WE ARE ESCAPED

Psalm 124

[1]If it had not been the LORD
    who was on our side,
    let Israel now say —
[2]if it had not been the LORD who
    was on our side,
    when men rose up against us,
[3]then they would have swallowed us
    up alive,
    when their anger was kindled
    against us;
[4]then the flood would have swept
    us away,
    the torrent would have gone over
    us;
[5]then over us would have gone
    the raging waters.

[6]Blessed be the LORD,
    who has not given us
    as prey to their teeth!
[7]We have escaped as a bird
    from the snare of the fowlers;
    the snare is broken,
    and we have escaped!

[8]Our help is in the name of the
    LORD,
    who made heaven and earth.

This is characteristically the psalm of deliverance. Scholars have suggested that it may be connected with the time when the Jews came back to Jerusalem and began to rebuild the shattered walls of the city. Then indeed their enemies did rise against them and try to hinder God's work (cp. *Nehemiah* 4:7-23). See p above.

Is there any man who has not had some great deliverance in his life? It may be that God preserved us in some time of danger; it may be that in sickness God led us back from the gates of death; or when we were nearly making shipwreck of life by falling to some grave temptation God held us back. Even if nothing as memorable as that has happened to us, at least we have been brought through all the chances and changes of life to this present hour. Like the psalmist we can say, our help is in the name of the Lord.

For meditation: *when I think of all that God has done for me: when I realise that hitherto the Lord has helped me: how can I face the future with fear?*

O GIVE THANKS

Psalm 136 (various verses)

[1]O give thanks to the LORD,
     for he is good,
          for his steadfast love endures for ever. ...

[4]to him who alone does great won-
          ders...
[5]to him who by understanding made
          the heavens. ...
[6]to him who spread out the earth
          upon the waters...

[10]to him who smote the first-born of
          Egypt...
[11]and brought Israel out from among
          them...

[23]It is he who remembered us in our
          low estate...
[24]and rescued us from our foes...
[25]he who gives food to all flesh...

[26]O give thanks to the God of heaven,
     for his steadfast love endures for
          ever.

The group of psalms from 113 to 118 are known to the Jews as the 'Hallel'. 'Hallel' literally means 'Praise God' and these psalms are so known because they were psalms of praise. This psalm is known as the 'Great Hallel' because it is the greatest of all songs of praise.

The psalmist thinks of God in three different spheres.

(1) God in nature(vv1-9). It is as if God had written his signature across the universe. Can we look at the wonders of the world without thinking of God, the maker and sustainer of them all?

(2) He thinks of God in history (vv10-22). In his mind's eye the psalmist surveys the history of his nation and sees in it repeatedly the delivering hand of God. As we look back across life, we too may see our days bound together by the golden thread of God's love: we too can say, 'Here and here and here God helped me.'

(3) He thinks of God in providence (vv23-6). The very food we eat comes to us from God. Our danger is that, because some of God's gifts come to us with unfailing regularity, we so easily take them for granted. Without God we could not live.

A prayer: *O God, you have made me and I am yours: you have redeemed me and I am doubly yours. Help me to love you with heart and soul and mind.*

148

GOD EVERYWHERE

Psalm 139: 1-7, 13-14

[1]O LORD, thou has searched
me and known me!
[2]Thou knowest when I sit down and
when I rise up;
thou discernest my thoughts
from afar.
[3]Thou searchest out my path and
my lying down,
and art acquainted with all my
ways.
[4]Even before a word is on my
tongue,
lo, O LORD, thou knowest it altogether.
[5]Thou dost beset me behind and
before,
and layest thy hand upon me.
[6]Such knowledge is too wonderful
for me;
it is high, I cannot attain it.

[7]Whither shall I go from thy Spirit?
Or whither shall I flee from thy
presence?...

[13]For thou didst form my inward
parts,
thou didst knit me together in
my mother's womb.
[14]I praise thee, for thou art fearful
and wonderful.
Wonderful are thy works!
Thou knowest me right well... .

Nothing in literature has such a sense of the universal presence of
God as this psalm. In the old days, before the world had been ex-
plored, men used to write on their maps, 'Here be burning fiery
sands' — 'Here be dragons' — 'Here be fearful things'; but this
psalmist writes all over the map of his world, 'Here is *God*.'

What is our reaction to this psalm? Does it fill our hearts with
terror? In this world there is no escape from God. There is nowhere
for a man to hide from the God who is everywhere. For the man
who has sin to conceal that is a terrible thought. Does it fill our
hearts with joy? If we love God and walk with him, we shall rejoice that nothing in the world can separate us from God.

To think about: *do I remember that God hears all my words,
sees all my actions, is aware of even my inmost thoughts?*

THE GREAT DOXOLOGY

Psalm 145: 1-3,13-18

¹I will extol thee, my God
and King,
and bless thy name for ever and
ever.
²Every day I will bless thee,
and praise thy name for ever and
ever.
³Great is the LORD, and greatly to be
praised,
and his greatness is unsearchable.
¹³... The LORD is faithful in all his
words,
and gracious in all his deeds.
¹⁴The LORD upholds all who are falling,
and raises up all who are bowed
down.
¹⁵The eyes of all look to thee,
and thou givest them their food
in due season.
¹⁶Thou openest thy hand,
thou satisfiest the desire of every
living thing.
¹⁷The LORD is just in all his ways,
and kind in all his doings.
¹⁸The LORD is near to all who call
upon him,
to all who call upon him in truth.

This is another of the alphabetical psalms. To the Jews it was one of the most precious. It was recited twice at the morning service of the synagogue; and once at the evening service. In the early Christian church it was specially used at the Lord's Supper, because of the appropriateness of verses 15 and 16.

It seems to meditate upon the qualities of God. (1) There is the recurring thought of the majesty of God (vv1-7,10-13). The Jew was always impressed with the sheer greatness of God; and, as modern science has shown us, the vastness of the world, the greatness of God, the creator and sustainer, have become ever plainer to see. (2) There is the thought of the graciousness of God. It is amazing how over and over again the psalms couple together the greatness and the graciousness of God. The greatness is not the greatness of a tyrant but of one in whose heart is love. (3) The psalm stresses the fidelity of God (vv19-21). The psalmist is certain that God will not fail those who put their trust in him.

To think about: *Is there enough sheer, joyous gratitude in my religion?*

THE WISDOM OF ISRAEL

(Selected readings in the book of Proverbs)

Proverbs is the distilled essence of the practical wisdom of Israel. In the days when the *Proverbs* came into being, books were scarce and expensive to buy. Printing had not yet been invented. Therefore wisdom could not be put into a form where it was readily available for thousands of people to buy. It is, in fact, interesting to note that the Hebrew word for instruction is *Mishnah*, which means repetition. A thing was learned by the master saying it and the pupil repeating it again and again until he knew it by heart. Thus it was essential that knowledge should be concentrated into forms that might be easily memorised. That explains the characteristics of the *Proverbs*. Almost every verse falls into two parallel halves, the second half repeating or developing the thought of the first.

In the *Proverbs* we have the concentrated, practical wisdom of Israel, put into a pithy, easily remembered form.

Why is *Proverbs* largely disconnected? The Hebrews had a strange view of preaching. They believed that a preacher, instead of lingering on one subject for any length of time, should move quickly from subject to subject, lest he weary his hearers. So they described preaching by the word *Charaz* which is the same word as describes stringing beads. *Proverbs* is like a string of pearls of wisdom. That very fact makes it difficult to comment adequately in the short space available to us; all that we can do is to pick out the leading thoughts and meditate upon them in the hope we too may draw from them wisdom for living.

THE SOURCES OF KNOWLEDGE

Proverbs 1:1-8

¹The proverbs of Solomon, son of
David, king of Israel:
²That men may know wisdom and
instruction,
understand words of insight,
³receive instruction in wise dealing,
righteousness, justice and equity;
⁴that prudence may be given to the
simple,
knowledge and discretion to the
youth —
⁵the wise man also may hear and
increase in learning,
and the man of understanding
acquire skill,
⁶to understand a proverb and a
figure,
the words of the wise and their
riddles.
⁷The fear of the LORD is the beginning of knowledge;
fools despise wisdom and instruction.
⁸Hear, my son, you father's instruction,
and reject not your mother's
teaching... .

In verses 7 and 8 the writer of the *Proverbs* shows us the sources
from which wisdom comes.

(1) From instruction. The greatest barrier to wisdom is the
unteachable spirit. The wisest man is he who is prepared to listen.

(2) We get wisdom from our parents. Young people often re-
sent guidance and control. If we are young let us remember that
our parents have come through life and know the dangers and pitfalls.

(3) We get wisdom from God. The fear of the Lord is the beginning of wisdom. The word fear does not mean a cringing, abject
terror, but respect, reverence, the recognition of the wisdom and
the greatness of God. God speaks to us by our consciences, by his
Spirit, in the pages of his book, in the voice of those who are his
servants. Have we learnt that reverence and humility which says,
speak Lord, for your servant is listening.

A prayer: *O God, give me the spirit of humility. May I be ready
to confess and admit my own ignorance and limitations.
Make me a good learner.*

RESISTING TEMPTATION

Proverbs 1:10-19

[10]My son, if sinners entice you,
    do not consent.
[11]If they say, "Come with us, let us
    lie in wait for blood,
    let us wantonly ambush the in-
    nocent;
[12]like Sheol let us swallow them alive
    and whole, like those who go
    down to the Pit;
[13]we shall find all precious goods,
    we shall fill our houses with spoil;
[14]throw in your lot among us,
    we will all have one purse" —
[15]my son, do not walk in the way
    with them,
    hold back your foot from their
    paths;
[16]for their feet run to evil,
    and they make haste to shed
    blood.
[17]For in vain is a net spread
    in the sight of any bird;
[18]but these men lie in wait for their
    own blood,
    they set an ambush for their own
    lives.
[19]Such are the ways of all who get
    gain by violence;
    it takes away the life of its pos-
    sessors.

This passage stresses the importance of being able to say no. Many people fall into wrong ways simply because they are afraid to be different from others. R L Stevenson once advised young people, stop saying amen to what the world says, and keep your soul alive.

It shows also that much of the world's sinning is due to greed. If we could free ourselves from the spirit of covetousness we should seldom go astray. The art of life is to do the best with the resources we have.

It stresses the importance of knowledge. The bird will never fall into the net when it knows that it is there. An instructed person has a far better chance of being safe. Parents and teachers should see that young people are warned against the pitfalls of life. How tragic it would be if some young person came to us some day and said, I should not have been in this trouble if you had only told me!

THE WAYS TO WISDOM

Proverbs 3:1-2,5-10

> [1]My son, do not forget my teach-
> ing,
>> but let your heart keep my com-
>> mandments;
> [2]for length of days and years of life
>> and abundant welfare will they
>> give you. ...
> [5]Trust in the LORD with all your
>> heart,
>> and do not rely on your own in-
>> sight.
> [6]In all your ways acknowledge him,
>> and he will make straight your
>> paths.
> [7]Be not wise in your own eyes;
>> fear the LORD, and turn away
>> from evil.
> [8]It will be healing to your flesh
>> and refreshment to your bones.
> [9]Honour the LORD with your sub-
>> stance
>> and with the first fruits of all
>> your produce;
> [10]then your barns will be filled with
>> plenty,
>> and your vats will be bursting
>> with wine.

Here we find the qualities which will bring a man happiness and peace.

He must have a retentive mind (vv1 and 2). When John Newton looked back on his young days and remembered the times when God had spoken to him, all he could say was, 'I forgot: I so soon forgot.' We shall avoid the danger of forgetting if at the beginning of each day we make a habit of thinking about God.

He must combine the love of truth and the love of mercy (vv3 and 4). Sometimes a man may use the truth in a cruel way. There is a prayer of Thomas Aquinas, 'Set a watch, O Lord, upon our tongues, that we may never speak the cruel word which is untrue, or being true, is not the whole truth, or being wholly true, is merciless.'

He must have trust in God (vv5 and 6). We were never asked to meet life alone.

He must have humility (vv7 and 8). It is the man who knows his own ignorance who is on the way to being wise and the man who knows his own weakness who will find the strength that is made perfect in that weakness.

THE TREASURES OF WISDOM

Proverbs 3:11-17

¹¹My son, do not despise the LORD's
discipline
or be weary of his reproof,
¹²for the LORD reproves him whom
he loves,
as a father the son in whom he
delights.

¹³Happy is the man who finds wis-
dom,
and the man who gets understanding,
¹⁴for the gain from it is better than
gain from silver
and its profit better than gold.
¹⁵She is more precious than jewels,
and nothing you desire can com-
pare with her.
¹⁶Long life is in her right hand;
in her left hand are riches and
honour.
¹⁷Her ways are ways of pleasantness,
and all her paths are peace.

Verses 11 and 12: the discipline of God. If a man sins he will suffer for it. But the discipline of God is inflicted in love and never
in anger. Our first feeling should not be resentment; we should
ask humbly, 'What is this experience meant to teach me?'

Verses 13-20: the treasures of wisdom. Wisdom gives a man true
wealth. The man who is wise has a gift which no earthly riches can
buy.

Wisdom gives a man true length of life. The value of a life lies
not in its length, but in its contribution to the world. 'We live
in deeds, not years.'

Wisdom gives happiness and peace. The right way is the only
way to a happiness which will last and to a peace which nothing
can destroy.

A prayer: *grant me, O God, that wisdom which will make me
truly rich and truly happy and which will give me life indeed.*

THE FORBIDDEN THINGS

Proverbs 6:6,10-11,16-18

⁶Go to the ant, O sluggard;
    consider her ways and be wise.

¹⁰A little sleep, a little slumber,
    a little folding of the hands to
      rest,
¹¹and poverty will come upon you
    like a vagabond,
    and want like an armed man.

¹⁶There are six things which the
    Lᴏʀᴅ hates,
    seven which are an abomination
      to him:
¹⁷haughty eyes, a lying tongue,
    and hands that shed innocent
      blood,
¹⁸a heart that devises wicked plans,
    feet that make haste to run to
      evil... .

Verses 6-11 warn against laziness. Hard work is the coin with which all worthwhile things are paid for. George Eliot speaks of 'hating all false work and loving true'.

Verses 12-15 warn against the mischievous spirit. There is a kind of person whose whole attitude invites one to think of life flippantly and frivolously, making a mockery and a jest of sacred things. God will not hold him guiltless who encourages or teaches others to sin.

Let us read again verses 16-18 and examine ourselves in the light of the seven things God hates. In particular, the last of them — sowing discord among brothers. We are not unaware of the sin of the tongue which loves gossip and is glad to spread idle rumours and slanderous tales. There is no sin which causes more damage to the Christian fellowship and more heartbreak to others.

A prayer: *O God, where there is discord help me to sow peace.*

THE CHAIN OF WISDOM

Proverbs 8:11-16, 19-20

> [11]for wisdom is better than jewels,
>> and all that you may desire can-
>> not compare with her.
>
> [12]I, wisdom, dwell in prudence,
>> and I find knowledge and discre-
>> tion.
>
> [13]The fear of the LORD is hatred of
>> evil.
>
> Pride and arrogance and the way of
>> evil
>
> and perverted speech I hate.
>
> [14]I have counsel and sound wisdom,
>> I have insight, I have strength.
>
> [15]By me kings reign,
>> and rulers decree what is just;
>
> [16]by me princes rule,
>> and nobles govern the earth. ...
>
> [19]My fruit is better than gold, even
>> fine gold,
>
> and my yield than choice silver.
>
> [20]I walk in the way of righteousness,
>> in the paths of justice,

Here wisdom makes her great claims to honour. She gives a man prudence and knowledge (v12). Every new situation in life brings its problems and difficulties. It is the wisdom given by God which enables a man to solve the problems and conquer difficulties. Wisdom teaches a man that there is no such thing as a hopeless situation.

Wisdom gives a man counsel (v14). There are certain people to whom we instinctively turn for advice when we are bewildered and perplexed. The man who has found the wisdom of God not only directs his own life but can also have the privilege of helping others to find the right way.

Wisdom enables men to rule (vv15 and 16). Kings and statesmen may control the lives of their subjects but every one of us has an influence on someone's life. It is only in the wisdom of God that our influence can point men on the upward way.

Wisdom keeps a man in the right way (v20). The easiest way to avoid getting lost is to follow someone who knows the road. If we follow the guidance wisdom gives, we shall come in safety and honour to our journey's end.

THE INSTRUMENT OF GOD

Proverbs 8:22-7, 35-6

²²The LORD created me at the begin-
ning of his work,
the first of his acts of old.
²³Ages ago I was set up,
at the first, before the beginning
of the earth.
²⁴When there were no depths I was
brought forth,
when there were no springs
abounding with water.
²⁵Before the mountains had been
shaped,
before the hills, I was brought
forth;
²⁶before he had made the earth with
its fields,
or the first of the dust of the
world.
²⁷When he established the heavens,
I was there,
when he drew a circle on the
face of the deep... .
³⁵For he who find me finds life
and obtains favour from the LORD;
³⁶but he who misses me injures him-
self;
all who hate me love death.

This is one of the sources of the prologue of St John's Gospel. John says that the Word was God's instrument in creation and that nothing was made without the Word (*John* 1:3). Now the Greek word *logos*, which John uses, means both *word* and *reason*; and *reason* is the same as *wisdom*.

In our passage from *Proverbs* God's wisdom is pictured as God's right hand, his instrument in the creation of the world. We have only to look at the world to see the marvellous order that is in it. Everything moves with amazing accuracy. That is so, says the writer of the *Proverbs* and John after him, because at the very heart of it there is the wisdom and the reason of God: in the design of the world we see the very nature and character of God.

When we look abroad upon the world in which we live and see its beauty and bounty, it should lift up our hearts to the power, the wisdom and the utter trustworthiness of the God who is the maker and creator of it all.

A prayer: *let your wisdom take possession of me, O God, that into my life there may come the order and beauty of your creation.*

THE IMPORTANCE OF WORDS

Proverbs 10:11-14, 18-19

[11]The mouth of the righteous is a
fountain of life,
but the mouth of the wicked conceals violence.
[12]Hatred stirs up strife,
but love covers all offences.
[13]On the lips of him who has understanding wisdom is found,
but a rod is for the back of him
who lacks sense.
[14]Wise men lay up knowledge,
but the babbling of a fool brings
ruin near. ...
[18]He who conceals hatred has lying
lips,
and he who utters slander is a
fool.
[19]When words are many, transgression is not lacking,
but he who restrains his lips is
prudent.

This passage is indeed like a disconnected string of pearls; but through it all the thought recurs of the importance of the tongue.

The good man speaks words which have in them life (v11). The Greeks talked about 'winged words'. Words wing their way into men's hearts and minds and bring either hurt or healing, encouragement to good or enticement to evil.

The good man speaks words which are wise (v13). If we do not think before we speak, or if we let impulse and passion sweep us into uncontrolled speaking, we shall inevitably say foolish things.

The tongue of the fool speaks slander (v18). Many a man or woman who would never dream of stealing a person's material possessions thinks nothing of stealing his good name and reputation by repeating the malicious tale: and that is the worst theft of all.

There is more value sometimes in silence, than in speech (v19). It was said of a wise man who was a linguist that his greatest gift was that he could keep silent in seven different languages!

The words of the wise are like food. Through them others find strength for life's way.

A prayer: *O God, teach me when to speak and when to keep silent. May my words be your words.*

UPRIGHT IN THEIR WAY

Proverbs 11:24-9

²⁴One man gives freely, yet grows all
    the richer;
  another withholds what he
    should give, and only suffers
    want.
²⁵A liberal man will be enriched,
  and one who waters will himself
    be watered.
²⁶The people curse him who holds
    back grain,
  but a blessing is on the head of
    him who sells it.
²⁷He who diligently seeks good seeks
    favour,
  but evil comes to him who searches for it.
²⁸He who trusts in his riches will
    wither,
  but the righteous will flourish
    like a green leaf.
²⁹He who troubles his household will
    inherit wind,
  and the fool will be servant to
    the wise.

Verse 24 foreshadows the teaching of Jesus. He who hoards his life will lose it; but he who spends it for God and men will find it. 'What I gave, I kept; what I kept, I lost.'

No one ever lost by being generous (vv25 and 26). God gives to all men generously. He is our great example.

There is no security in material things (vv28). 'Lay up for yourselves treasure in heaven,' said our Lord.

To cause trouble in one's own home is the act of a fool (v29). Sometimes in our homes we are fretful and complaining, grumbling and irritable, in a way that we would never dare to be with strangers. Remember that Jesus is an unseen but ever present guest in our homes.

Thought for the day: *to what extent does my happiness depend on material things?*

THE VALUABLE VIRTUES

Proverbs 12:17-25

[17]He who speaks the truth gives
honest evidence,
but a false witness utters deceit.
[18]There is one whose rash words are
like sword thrusts,
but the tongue of the wise brings
healing.
[19]Truthful lips endure for ever,
but a lying tongue is but for a
moment.
[20]Deceit is in the heart of those who
devise evil,
but those who plan good have
joy.
[21]No ill befalls the righteous,
but the wicked are filled with
trouble.
[22]Lying lips are an abomination to
the LORD,
but those who act faithfully are
his delight.
[23]A prudent man conceals his knowledge,
but fools proclaim their folly.
[24]The hand of the diligent will rule,
while the slothful will be put to
forced labour.
[25]Anxiety in a man's heart weighs
him down,
but a good word makes him glad.

Verses 17-23 are the glorification of truth. People swerve from the truth for two main reasons. Sometimes we fail through sheer carelessness. Dr Johnson held that from his earliest years a child should be compelled to watch deliberately that he spoke the truth, because, he said, it is more from sheer carelessness than from any deliberation that men twist the truth. Before we make a statement it is good to ask ourselves, do I know for certain that this is true?

Verse 24 preaches the gospel of work. The prizes of life do not fall into our laps without any effort of our own. It is to him who overcomes that the promises are made.

Verse 25 stresses the value of a word of encouragement. The world is full of people who are fighting a hard battle; it is a gracious, Christlike thing to speak a word which will lift up their hearts.

THE FEAR OF THE LORD

Proverbs 14:12, 26-31

> [12]There is a way which seems right
> to a man,
>> but its end is the way to death. ...
>
> [26]In the fear of the LORD one has
> strong confidence,
>> and his children will have a
>> refuge.
>
> [27]The fear of the LORD is a fountain
> of life,
>> that one may avoid the snares of
>> death.
>
> [28]In a multitude of people is the glory
> of a king,
>> but without people a prince is
>> ruined.
>
> [29]He who is slow to anger has great
> understanding,
>> but he who has a hasty temper
>> exalts folly.
>
> [30]A tranquil mind gives life to the
> flesh,
>> but passion makes the bones rot.
>
> [31]He who oppresses a poor man in-
> sults his Maker,
>> but he who is kind to the needy
>> honours him.

Verse 12: what is it that makes a man take the wrong way under the delusion that it is the right way?

Verses 26-35 are scattered with great thoughts. The fear of the Lord (vv27-8) is a necessity for the good life. The fear of the Lord is the deep reverence of one who knows himself in the presence of the all-good and the all-wise.

The wise man is the man whose temper is under control (v29).

Envy is a canker which takes all the soundness out of life (v30).

The surest way to unhappiness is to envy others. The true man will be glad when he sees the good fortune of others.

A nation's true wealth is in righteousness (v34).

For meditation: *what motives move me to any course of action? Can I honestly say that my first desire is to find out God's will?*

THE RIGHTEOUS MAN

Proverbs 15:1-5, 13-17

[1]A soft answer turns away
wrath,
but a harsh word stirs up anger.
[2]The tongue of the wise dispenses
knowledge,
but the mouths of fools pour out
folly.
[3]The eyes of the LORD are in every
place,
keeping watch on the evil and
the good.
[4]A gentle tongue is a tree of life,
but perverseness in it breaks the
spirit.
[5]A fool despises his father's instruction,
but he who heeds admonition is
prudent. ...
[13]A glad heart makes a cheerful
countenance,
but by sorrow of heart the spirit
is broken.
[14]The mind of him who has understanding seeks knowledge,
but the mouths of fools feed on
folly.
[15]All the days of the afflicted are
evil,
but a cheerful heart has a con-
tinual feast.
[16]Better is a little with the fear of the
LORD
than great treasure and trouble
with it.
[17]Better is a dinner of herbs where
love is
than a fatted ox and hatred with
it.

THE RIGHTEOUS MAN (continued)

There are certain main thoughts in the precepts of this passage.

The characteristics of the tongue of the wise man. The wise man knows that to answer bitterness with bitterness begets bitterness; but a kindly answer to an unkind word is a true conquest (v1). Perverse speaking can cause nothing but trouble (vv4 and 7). Here is an old jingle with a wealth of truth in it:

> If wisdom's ways you wisely seek,
> Five things observe with care —
> Of whom you speak, to whom you speak,
> And why, and when and where.

The wise man willingly listens to instruction and accepts rebuke (vv5,10 and 12). That needs humility. Many a man would have been saved much trouble if he had admitted that he had made a mistake.

A happy heart makes a happy life (vv13 and 15). The man who has the joy that no man takes from him is independent of circumstances; he carries his joy with him wherever he goes.

Nothing can take the place of love (v17). The humblest meal becomes sweet if love flavours it.

A prayer: *O God, if I have someone to love me, help me to remember that I have the most precious thing in all the world.*

To take with us today: *'a soft answer turns away wrath' (v1).*

THE HEART OF MAN

Proverbs 16:1-4, 7-9

[1]The plans of the mind belong
to man,
but the answer of the tongue is
from the LORD.
[2]All the ways of a man are pure in
his own eyes,
but the LORD weighs the spirit.
[3]Commit your work to the LORD,
and your plans will be established.
[4]The LORD has made everything for
its purpose,
even the wicked for the day of
trouble. ...
[7]When a man's ways please the
LORD,
he makes even his enemies to be
at peace with him.
[8]Better is a little with righteousness
than great revenues with injustice.
[9]A man's mind plans his way,
but the LORD directs his steps.

The importance of a man's inmost thoughts is emphasised here. Our outward deeds may be a model of piety and respectability; but it is the heart that is really important. In the Sermon on the Mount Jesus teaches that it is not enough merely to abstain from sinning; we must not even want to sin.

If a man in his heart of hearts desires to do wrong things and yet compels himself to do right it means that there is a perpetual struggle between his will and his desires. So long as his will is strong enough his actions will be good: but the will is like a leash which may snap at any moment; and so long as the desires and the will are in conflict there can be no safety. Hence the need for complete inward cleansing which only the love and friendship of Christ can perform.

A prayer: *'Almighty God, to whom all hearts are open, all desires known, and from whom no secrets are hid: cleanse the thoughts of our hearts by the inspiration of your Holy Spirit that we may perfectly love you and worthily magnify your Holy Name.'*

THE EXCELLENCE OF LOVE

Proverbs 17:1, 8-13

> [1]Better is a dry morsel with
> quiet
> than a house full of feasting with
> strife. ...
> [8]A bribe is like a magic stone in the
> eyes of him who gives it;
> wherever he turns he prospers.
> [9]He who forgives an offence seeks
> love,
> but he who repeats a matter
> alienates a friend.
> [10]A rebuke goes deeper into a man of
> understanding
> than a hundred blows into a fool.
> [11]An evil man seeks only rebellion,
> and a cruel messenger will be
> sent against him.
> [12]Let a man meet a she-bear robbed
> of her cubs,
> rather than a fool in his folly.
> [13]If a man returns evil for good,
> evil will not depart from his
> house.

A home may be poor, but love makes it rich. If a house shelters divided hearts there is no happiness in it (v1).

Unkindness is not only an insult to man; it is an insult to God (v5). All men are the sons of God: therefore to fail to help a fellow man in need is to fail to help God. To rejoice at the misfortune of another is to rejoice at something which has hurt the heart of God.

A gift is like a jewel (v8). And it is twice blessed because it gives joy to him who has received it and happiness to him who gave it.

The man who knows what love is will be able to forgive and forget a wrong that has been done (v9).

A prayer: *O God, give me that love which in seeking the happiness of others will bring happiness to myself.*

A suggestion: *read Paul's 'Hymn of Love' (1 Corinthians 13).*

THINGS TO CEASE FROM

Proverbs 20:1-4, 9-11

[1]Wine is a mocker, strong
    drink a brawler;
    and whoever is led astray by it is
    not wise.
[2]The dread wrath of a king is like
    the growling of a lion;
    he who provokes him to anger
    forfeits his life.
[3]It is an honour for a man to keep
    aloof from strife;
    but every fool will be quarrelling.
[4]The sluggard does not plough in the
    autumn;
    he will seek at harvest and have
    nothing. ...
[9]Who can say, "I have made my
    heart clean;
    I am pure from my sin?"
[10]Diverse weights and diverse meas-
    ures
    are both alike an abomination to
    the LORD.
[11]Even a child makes himself known
    by his acts,
    whether what he does is pure
    and right.

We are warned against intemperance (v1); against meddling (v3); against too much search for comfort (v4); and unfair dealing (v10).

The test is the test of conduct (v11).

Here is a challenge. How can we spread Christianity and attract men and women into the church? By proving that Christianity produces the finest men and women. Are we more diligent, more honest, more conscientious workers than those who are not professing Christians? If we are employers or in control of others are we juster, fairer, more generous than the non-Christian? Are we kinder, lovelier, more winsome than those outside the church?

A prayer:
Send down thy likeness from above,
    And let this my adorning be;
Clothe me with wisdom, patience, love,
With lowliness and purity.
    Than gold and pearls more precious far,
And brighter than the morning star.

THE JUST MAN AND THE WICKED

Proverbs 24:15-20

¹⁵Lie not in wait as a wicked man
against the dwelling of the
righteous;
do not violence to his home;
¹⁶for a righteous man falls seven
times, and rises again;
but the wicked are overthrown
by calamity.
¹⁷Do not rejoice when your enemy
falls,
and let not your heart be glad
when he stumbles;
¹⁸lest the LORD see it, and be dis-
pleased,
and turn away his anger from
him.
¹⁹Fret not yourself because of evil-
doers,
and be not envious of the wicked;
²⁰for the evil man has no future;
the lamp of the wicked will be
put out.

Here are contrasts between the just man and the wicked.

There is a certain undefeatable quality about the good man (v16). It has been said that a saint is not a man who never falls, but one who stubbornly rises again. It has also been said that Christianity is not so much concerned with where a man is, as with the direction in which he is facing. To the end of the day, may our faces be turned towards God.

The good man must never find pleasure in the misfortunes even of his enemies (v17,18). He must have that unconquerable love which never wishes his bitterest enemy anything but good.

The good man will not fret himself because the wicked prosper (v19,20). He will leave the matter in the hands of God, for what is a brief day of worldy prosperity compared with the joy of eterni-ty?

A prayer: *grant to me, also, O God, the power which will enable me to rise and press on, no matter how often I may fall.*

WARNINGS TO THE WISE

Proverbs 28:20-26

²⁰A faithful man will abound with
blessings,
but he who hastens to be rich will
not go unpunished.
²¹To show partiality is not good;
but for a piece of bread a man
will do wrong.
²²A miserly man hastens after wealth,
and does not know that want will
come upon him.
²³He who rebukes a man will after-
ward find more favour
than he who flatters with his
tongue.
²⁴He who robs his father or his
mother
and says, "That is no transgression,"
is the companion of a man who
destroys.
²⁵A greedy man stirs up strife,
but he who trusts in the LORD
will be enriched.
²⁶He who trusts in his own mind is
a fool;
but he who walks in wisdom will
be delivered.

As so often, the writer of the *Proverbs* warns us against the things
which can bring life to ruin.

He warns us against the desire to get rich quickly (vv20,22). The
important questions about a man's possessions are, how did he get
them? How does he use them?

He warns us against respect of persons (v21). It is true of some
people that the voice of their neighbours sounds more loudly in
their ears than the voice of God. Before God all men are equal
and no man's earthly status or prestige should hinder us from doing what is right.

He warns us against flattery (v23).

He warns us against robbing our parents (v24). We may rob our
parents not only of material things — and we do so rob them when
we make no attempt to repay them for all they spent to give us
our chance in life — but we can also rob them of the respect, the
obedience, the love, which is their due.

He warns us against pride and over self-confidence (v26). Pride
always goes before a fall.

WHERE THERE IS NO VISION, THE PEOPLE PERISH

Proverbs 29:18-23

> [18]Where there is no prophecy the
> people cast off restraint,
> but blessed is he who keeps the
> law.
> [19]By mere words a servant is not
> disciplined,
> for though he understands, he
> will not give heed.
> [20]Do you see a man who is hasty in
> his words?
> There is more hope for a fool
> than for him.
> [21]He who pampers his servant from
> childhood,
> will in the end find him his
> heir.
> [22]A man of wrath stirs up strife,
> and a man given to anger causes
> much transgression.
> [23]A man's pride will bring him low,
> but he who is lowly in spirit will
> obtain honour.

There are two translations of this. The first, as given here, is from the *Authorised Version*. It means two things. Where men have no pattern for life sent by God, life comes to disaster. No one would think of building a ship or constructing a machine without a plan. If we would build a good life we need to receive the design of it from God, who gives his pattern to those who are prepared to listen to his voice.

Where men's thoughts are purely earthbound, disaster must follow. To live life on the assumption that only this world and this life matter, means losing everything that makes life worth while.

But the second translation is equally suggestive — 'Where there is no *bridle* the people perish.' Men need restraint. We get that restraint from the voice of conscience, and from the memory of the presence of Christ.

Think about and use as a prayer:
> *Be Thou my vision, O Lord of my heart;*
> *Naught be all else to me, save that Thou art —*
> *Thou my best thought, by day or by night.*
> *Waking or sleeping, Thy presence my light.*

FOUR KINDS OF PEOPLE

Proverbs 30:7-14

⁷Two things I ask of thee;
    deny them not to me before I die:
⁸Remove far from me falsehood and
      lying;
    give me neither poverty nor
    riches;
    feed me with the food that is
    needful for me,
⁹lest I be full, and deny thee,
    and say, "Who is the LORD?"
  or lest I be poor, and steal,
    and profane the name of my
    God. ...
¹¹There are those who curse their fathers
    and do not bless their mothers.
¹²There are those who are pure in
    their own eyes
    but are not cleansed of their filth.
¹³There are those — how lofty are
    their eyes,
    how high their eyelids lift!
¹⁴There are those whose teeth are
    swords,
    whose teeth are knives,
  to devour the poor from off the
    earth,
    the needy from among men.

The writer of the *Proverbs* has two prayers. First, he prays to be kept from vanity and lies, which separates us from God, for only the pure in heart shall see God. And he prays to be kept from too much prosperity. We often think we can do without God when things are going well and call upon him only when we are in trouble. That is a shameful thing.

In verses 11-14 four kinds of people are described and condemned. Those who do not realise their own sin and folly. Those who are proud. Those who are selfishly cruel.

For self-examination: *do I fall within any of these classes? I had better be quite sure.*

171

THE PROPHETS

The study of the prophets has suffered because so many people have limited the work of the prophet to one particular function. We are apt to think of him as a man who *foretold* things before they happened. But the prophets were not nearly so much as *fore*-tellers as they were *forth*-tellers. They declared God's will in any time of decision, God's verdict on any action, God's policy in any undertaking. Because of that they were bound to foretell the *consequences* of the deeds of men and nations. But they seldom dealt in dates and times. Their message was, if you persist in such and such a course of action which is against the will of God, the consequences will be terrible; if you submit to the will of God the consequences will be happiness and peace. They were the conscience of the nation because they brought to the people the voice of God. In this section we are to read passages from some of the great prophets.

GOD LOOKS AT HIS WORLD

Isaiah 1:1-5

> 2Hear, O heavens, and give ear, O
> earth;
>> for the LORD has spoken:
>> "Sons have I reared and brought up,
>> but they have rebelled against
>>> me.
>
> 3The ox knows its owner,
>> and the ass its master's crib;
>> but Israel does not know,
>> my people does not understand."
>
> 4Ah, sinful nation,
>> a people laden with iniquity,
>> offspring of evildoers,
>> sons who deal corruptly!
>> They have forsaken the LORD,
>> they have despised the Holy One
>>> of Israel,
>> they are utterly estranged.
>
> 5Why will you still be smitten,
>> that you continue to rebel?
>> The whole head is sick,
>> and the whole heart faint.

What we think about God is very important. It makes all the difference to our outlook on life and to our way of meeting its trials and troubles.

But what God thinks of us is even more important. How does the world look from God's side? We all agree that something has gone wrong. But what is it? In this reading God speaks through the mouth of Isaiah. The people of Israel were God's people. They were his family which he had brought into being, and on which he had poured out his love. But they had turned against him, rejected his love, and taken life into their own hands to live it in their own way. They were spiritually sick, like a human body when the laws of health have been broken.

This diagnosis of the ills of Israel is true of the world today. Our civilisation also is sick. We often say it is because people have fallen away from the Christian faith. But what does this mean? It means that we have ignored or forgotten our true identity. We are the children of God, and, like the prodigal, we have turned our back on father and home. Our only hope is, like the prodigal also, to come to ourselves and return to the Father in penitence and seek his fellowship.

A prayer: *gracious Father, help us to realise that we are your children, and draw us by your grace into fellowship with you.*

THE ONLY TRUE WORSHIP

Isaiah 1:11-17

[11]"What to me is the multitude of
  your sacrifices?"
  says the LORD;
 I have had enough of burnt offerings of rams
 and the fat of fed beasts;
 I do not delight in the blood of
  bulls,
 or of lambs, or of he-goats.

[12]"When you come to appear before
  me,
  who requires of you
  this trampling of my courts?
[13]Bring no more vain offerings;
  incense is an abomination to me.
 New moon and sabbath and the
  calling of assemblies —
 I cannot endure iniquity and
  solemn assembly.
[14]Your new moons and your appointed feasts
  my soul hates;
 they have become a burden to me,
 I am weary of bearing them.
[15]When you spread forth your hands,
 I will hide my eyes from you;
 even though you make many
  prayers,
 I will not listen;
 your hands are full of blood.
[16]Wash yourselves; make yourselves
  clean;
  remove the evil of your doings
  from before my eyes;
  cease to do evil,
[17]learn to do good;
  seek justice,
  correct oppression;
  defend the fatherless,
  plead for the widow.

THE ONLY TRUE WORSHIP (continued)

The people meticulously observed their holy days, burned their incense and brought their offerings; but instead of pleasing God it was all an abomination to him because their lives were evil. Once again men were seeking to substitute ritual for conduct. And the cry of Isaiah is for justice.

Verse 17 tells what justice really means. The essence of it is that to seek justice is not to seek to safeguard one's own rights; it is to be intensely interested in the rights of others. Frequently when we say, 'All I want is justice', what we really mean is that all we want is to have our own rights conserved and our own just reward. That to Isaiah was not justice; it was selfishness.

Use as a prayer:
> *O give us hearts to love like Thee,*
> *Like Thee, O Lord, to grieve*
> *Far more for others' sins, than all*
> *The wrongs that we receive.*

THE LIGHT OF THE LORD

Isaiah 2:1-5

²It shall come to pass in the latter
          days
     that the mountain of the house
     of the LORD
   shall be established as the highest
     of the mountains,
     and shall be raised above the
     hills;
   and all the nations shall flow to it,
³and many peoples shall come,
     and say:
   "Come, let us go up to the moun-
     tain of the LORD,
    to the house of the God of Jacob;
   that he may teach us his ways
     and that we may walk in his
     paths."
   For out of Zion shall go forth the
     law,
     and the word of the LORD from
     Jerusalem.
⁴He shall judge between the nations,
     and shall decide for many peo-
     ples;
   and they shall beat their swords
     into ploughshares,
     and their spears into pruning
     hooks;
   nation shall not lift up sword
     against nation,
     neither shall they learn war any
     more.
⁵O house of Jacob,
     come, let us walk
     in the light of the LORD.

The Jews believed that since they were the chosen people of God they had been singled out for a special privileges. They looked for a day when the Gentiles would be wiped out or reduced to the status of slaves.

But Isaiah interpreted the conception of the chosen people in terms of a great responsibility. It was the task of Israel to lead men to God. He saw Israel's destiny not in a career of conquest but of missionary endeavour. He saw Jerusalem not as the centre of a world subdued by conquest but as the place to which all men would turn to learn of God.

No man ever really experiences the full content of Christianity until there comes into his heart the desire to share it with others.

THE VINEYARD OF THE LORD

Isaiah 5:1-4

¹Let me sing for my beloved
   a love song concerning his vine-
     yard:
   My beloved had a vineyard
   on a very fertile hill.
²He digged it and cleared it of
     stones,
     and planted it with choice vines;
     he built a watchtower in the midst
      of it,
     and hewed out a wine vat in it;
     and he looked for it to yield grapes,
     but it yielded wild grapes.
³And now, O inhabitants of Jeru-
     salem
   and men of Judah,
   judge, I pray you, between me
   and my vineyard.
⁴What more was there to do for my
     vineyard,
   that I have not done in it?
   When I looked for it to yield
     grapes,
   why did it yield wild grapes?

Often the Jews thought of themselves as the vineyard of the Lord. So God says to Israel, I have done everything that could possibly be done for you and yet you have not brought forth fruits to fit all this; therefore punishment must come.

How have we used the gifts of God? Someone wrote a terrible parable like this: Jesus was going down the city street one day and in a house he saw a young man feasting gluttonously and drinking recklessly. He said to him, 'Son, why do you live like that?' The young man replied, 'But I was a leper and you cleansed me. How else should I live?' Jesus went further and saw a girl with painted finery going down the street and a young man following her with the eyes of a hunter. He said to the young man, 'Son, why do you look at that girl like that?' And he answered, 'But I was blind and you made me able to see. How else should I look?' Jesus touched the girl on the shoulder and said, 'Daughter, why do you live a life on the streets like this?' She turned and answered, 'But I was a sinner and you forgave me my sins. How else should I live?'

Here were three people who had received wonderful gifts from Jesus but had failed to understand *why* they were given. How are we using the gifts that God has bestowed upon us?

THE VISION OF GOD

Isaiah 6:1-8

¹In the year that King Uzzi'ah died I saw the LORD sitting upon a throne, high and lifted up; and his train filled the temple. ²Above him stood the seraphim; each had six wings: with two he covered his face, and with two he covered his feet, and with two he flew. ³And one called to another and said:

"Holy, holy, holy is the LORD of
hosts;

the whole earth is full of his glory."

⁴And the foundation of the thresholds shook at the voice of him who called, and the house was filled with smoke. ⁵And I said: "Woe is me! For I am lost; for I am a man of unclean lips, and I dwell in the midst of a people of unclean lips; for my eyes have seen the King, the LORD of hosts!"

⁶Then flew one of the seraphim to me, having in his hand a burning coal which he had taken with tongs from the altar. ⁷And he touched my mouth, and said: "Behold, this has touched your lips; your guilt is taken away, and your sin forgiven." ⁸And I heard the voice of the Lord saying, "Whom shall I send, and who will go for us?" Then I said, "Here am I! Send me."

Where was Isaiah when he received the vision? In the house of God. Where are we more likely to meet God than in his house? Are we diligent in our church attendance?

In the presence of God Isaiah realised as never before his own sin. All religious experience must start with a sense of our own unworthiness. We never really find God until we realise our need of him.

The God who shows us our sin is the God who can also cleanse us.

Isaiah left God's presence with a task to perform. God is still seeking people who will say, with Isaiah, 'Here am I, send me.'

A thought: *the vision of God leads to hard work for him. The hymn-writer says, 'They who fain would serve you best are conscious most of wrong within.' What does he mean? Does the experience of Isaiah throw anylight on the question?*

THE PRINCE TO COME

Isaiah 9:2-7

²The people who walked in dark-
ness
have seen a great light;
those who dwelt in a land of deep
darkness,
on them has light shined. ...
⁶For to us a child is born,
to us a son is given;
and the government will be upon
his shoulder,
and his name will be called
"Wonderful Counsellor, Mighty
God,
Everlasting Father, Prince of
Peace."
⁷Of the increase of his government
and of peace
there will be no end,
upon the throne of David, and over
his kingdom,
to establish it, and to uphold it
with justice and with righteousness
from this time forth and for evermore.
The zeal of the LORD of hosts will
do this.

Here is the prophet's dream of the king who was to come.

He was to be a Wonderful Counsellor (The two words go together: there should be no comma between them.) Jesus was that. People came to him asking 'What shall I do?' and he took their bewildered, broken lives and made then whole. He can do the same for us.

He was to be the Mighty God. Until Jesus came men could only guess and grope at what God was like; but when he came he declared, 'He who has seen me has seen the Father' (*John* 14:9).

His name was the Everlasting Father. The very word rather breathes love and grace. Into the majesty of God there comes this new gentleness of which men had scarcely dreamed. Now they could come like children to a father.

He was to be the Prince of Peace. The world had known a succession of conquerors who had wrought death and destruction, shattered houses, scorched fields, broken lives and hearts. But there would come one whose might was love and whose throne was a cross.

Far more wonderfully than he knew, the prophet's dream came true in Jesus Christ.

THEY SHALL NOT HURT

Isaiah 11:1-3,6,9

[1]There shall come forth a shoot
   from the stump of Jesse,
      and a branch shall grow out of
         his roots.
[2]And the Spirit of the LORD shall
      rest upon him,
      the spirit of wisdom and under-
         standing,
      the spirit of counsel and might,
      the spirit of knowledge and the
         fear of the LORD.
[3]And his delight shall be in the fear
      of the LORD ... .
[6]The wolf shall dwell with the lamb,
      and the leopard shall lie down
         with the kid,
      and the calf and the lion and the
         fatling together,
      and a little child shall lead them. ...
[9]They shall not hurt or destroy
      in all my holy mountain;
      for the earth shall be full of the
         knowledge of the LORD
      as the waters cover the sea.

A picture is drawn of a world at peace. In the age of God to come even the creatures which are instinctive enemies shall be at peace one with another.

Only by the coming of Christ into men's hearts can the world achieve such a peace. It is only in Christ that men discover that they are brothers. It is only Christ who can enable men to forgive. In one of his books Dr Weatherhead tells how the Turks once sacked an Armenian village. A Turkish officer came into a house and murdered both the parents and their family, except one girl whom he kept for himself. Later the girl escaped and became a nurse. Into the hospital one night was brought a Turkish officer wounded almost to death. It was the very man who had brought her so much sorrow and shame. She had only to neglect him a little and he would die; but she nursed him devotedly. When he came back to himself after weeks of nursing he recognised her. He asked her how she had ever managed to do what she had done for him in view of what he had done to her. She said she worshipped one who taught men to forgive, and told him something of Christianity. When she had finished he said, 'Tell me something more. If there is a religion like yours in this world I want it.'

A prayer: *O Christ, help me to forgive others as you have forgiven me.*

A VISION OF HOPE

Isaiah 26:1-6

[1]In that day the song will be
    sung in the land of Judah:
     "We have a strong city;
    he sets up salvation
    as walls and bulwarks.
[2]Open the gates,
    that the righteous nation which
     keeps faith
    may enter in.
[3]Thou dost keep him in perfect
     peace,
    whose mind is stayed on thee,
    because he trusts in thee.
[4]Trust in the LORD for ever,
    for the LORD God
    is an everlasting rock.
[5]For he has brought low
    the inhabitants of the height,
    the lofty city.
   He lays it low, lays it low to the
    ground,
    casts it to the dust.
[6]The foot tramples it,
    the feet of the poor,
    the steps of the needy."

The vision of a kingdom of peace and brotherhood has glimmered in the hearts of men through all the darkness and conflict of the world.

In Isaiah's mind it takes the form of a city with walls and bulwarks. It can come into being only through the salvation of God, not merely through human achievement and organisation. It is built by those whose hearts are ruled by God and whose lives are changed by his Spirit. The peace of the city will not come by the victory of one empire over others, but by the rule of God in the hearts of all. God's peace cannot be imposed from without. It is the fruit of righteousness, and has its springs in hearts that are stayed on God and find their security in his love. We are restless and antagonistic to one another because we have no real peace within. It is that peace we are called to seek. When we have it we can face the tumults around us without fear. George Matheson wrote of our human will,

It only stands unbent,
Amid the clashing strife,
When on Thy bosom it has leant
And found in Thee its life.

THE WAY OF GOD

Isaiah 35:1-6

[1]The wilderness and the dry
    land shall be glad,
  the desert shall rejoice and blos-
      som;
  like the crocus [2]it shall blossom
    abundantly,
  and rejoice with joy and singing. ...
[3]Strengthen the weak hands,
  and make firm the feeble knees.
[4]Say to those who are of a fearful
    heart,
  ''Be strong, fear not!
  Behold, your God
  will come with vengeance,
  with the recompense of God.
  He will come and save you.''
[5]Then the eyes of the blind shall be
    opened,
  and the ears of the deaf un-
    stopped;
[6]then shall the lame man leap like a
    hart,
  and the tongue of the dumb sing
    for joy.
  For waters shall break forth in the
    wilderness,
  and streams in the desert... .

Here is a vision of the world as it will be when God's loving rule is accepted by all men.

It will be a world of beauty. The Holy Spirit of God can make the barren life fruitful in all lovely things.

It will be a world of strength and healing. Someone said of Jesus that the greatest thing he did was that he went about 'making poor half-men whole'.

It will be a world refreshed. Many people in our generation are tired. There is a certain weariness of life. When John Wesley was over eighty he once said, 'For the last ten years I have not known what it is to feel tired.' Only the grace of God can enable men to pass the breaking point and not to break.

It will be a world of joy. Men will know the joy which no man can take from them.

A prayer: *help me, O God, to walk your way that I may know your joy and come in safety to my journey's end.*

OUR PART IN REVIVAL

Isaiah 40:1-4

¹Comfort, comfort my peo-
ple,
says your God.
²Speak tenderly to Jerusalem,
and cry to her
that her warfare is ended,
that her iniquity is pardoned,
that she has received from the
LORD's hand
double for all her sins.
³A voice cries:
"In the wilderness prepare the way
of the LORD,
make straight in the desert a
highway for our God.
⁴Every valley shall be lifted up,
and every mountain and hill be
made low;
the uneven ground shall become
level... .

This reading takes us back to the time when the exiles in Babylon were on the point of returning to Jerusalem.

There are two notes in the prophet's message. One is the note of comfort. The period of judgment is over; the time of healing and redemption has come. But there is also the note of challenge. The people must rise from their depression and face the long way home with all the labours and hazards of the road. They must make straight the paths and fill up the valleys and make a highway for God.

The picture comes from days when princes who made a journey had men going before them to prepare the way; but there is a message for us. The new world is of God's creation. The power and the will to create it come from his Spirit. But we must take action. There are crooked things to be made straight; there are conditions to be created in which men and women can be saved from frustration and despair. Wrong things in our own lives must be set right. God in his providence responds to that activity of faith and love.

Is there some work of preparation in which we can lend a hand?

A prayer: *O God, who works in us by your Spirit both to will and to do, help us to work out in practical service what you are working in us.*

THE POWER AND THE LOVE

Isaiah 40:6-11

[6]A voice says, "Cry!"
    And I said, "What shall I cry?"
    All flesh is grass,
        and all its beauty is like the flower
            of the field.
[7]The grass withers, the flower fades,
        when the breath of the LORD
            blows upon it;
        surely the people is grass.
[8]The grass withers, the flower fades;
        but the word of our God will
            stand for ever.
[9]Get you up to a high mountain,
        O Zion, herald of good tidings;
    lift up your voice with strength,
        O Jerusalem, herald of good tid-
            ings,
    lift it up, fear not;
    say to the cities of Judah,
        "Behold your God!"
[10]Behold, the Lord GOD comes with
            might,
        and his arm rules for him;
        behold, his reward is with him,
        and his recompense before him.
[11]He will feed his flock like a shep-
            herd,
        he will gather the lambs in his
            arms,
        he will carry them in his bosom,
        and gently lead those that are
            with young.

Verses 3 and 4 described what was done when a king signified that he would make a tour of the country. The roads were levelled out and the rough places were made smooth for his coming. Here is a picture of God as the coming king.

But in verse 11 there is the picture of God as the shepherd. Often on the roads of Palestine you might see the shepherd with a tired or injured lamb carried in his arms as we might carry a child.

Now in these two pictures the two great attributes of God are conjoined. The picture of God as king indicates God's power; the picture of God as shepherd tells us of God's love. God's love is backed by his power and must therefore be triumphant in the end.

WAITING UPON GOD

Isaiah 40:27-31

27Why do you say, O Jacob,
and speak, O Israel,
"My way is hid from the LORD,
and my right is disregarded by
my God"?
28Have you not known? Have you not
heard?

The LORD is the everlasting God,
the Creator of the ends of the
earth.
He does not faint or grow weary,
his understanding is unsearchable.
29He gives power to the faint,
and to him who has no might he
increases strength.
30Even youths shall faint and be
weary,
and young men shall fall ex-
hausted;
31but they who wait for the LORD
shall renew their strength,
they shall mount up with wings
like eagles,
they shall run and not be weary,
they shall walk and not faint.

Verses 25-8 tell us of the kind of God in whom we believe. His power upholds the universe.

Verses 29-31: that power is used to help the needy and to uphold the weak.

Verse 31: those who wait on God shall mount up with wings as eagles. It is said that the eagle is the only living creature which can look straight into the sun. This then means that if we wait on God there will be given to us tremendous moments of vision when we see God's glory fully displayed.

Again, those who wait on God shall run and not be weary. This means that if we wait on God we shall be enabled to make sustained and strenuous efforts in the emergencies of life.

Those who wait on God will walk and not faint. In the ordinary run of things, when nothing special is happening, but when the ordinary duties of life have to go on, the glory of God will be with us. That is the greatest promise of all.

To remember: *these promises are to those who 'wait upon the Lord'. How often do we wait upon him?*

THE CONDITIONS OF BLESSING

Isaiah 64:1,6-8

[1]O that thou wouldst rend the
heavens and come down,
that the mountains might quake
at thy presence... .
[6]We have all become like one who
is unclean,
and all our righteous deeds are
like a polluted garment.
We all fade like a leaf,
and our iniquities, like the wind,
take us away.
[7]There is no one that calls upon thy
name,
that bestirs himself to take hold
of thee;
for thou hast hid thy face from us,
and hast delivered us into the
hand of our iniquities.

It is God who brings in his kingdom, not we.

What are the conditions in which he is able to work? Jesus, we are told, could do no mighty works in his own town because of their unbelief. Isaiah says the same thing in other words, 'God works for him that waits for him.' Belief is essential. They that come to God must believe that he is.

But that is only the beginning. Belief in God, in the bible sense, means the faith that rests on God till we are quiet enough and passive enough for him to make his voice heard and his power victorious. But it means also the practice of thinking through our habits and our ideas in daily life to make sure that these are based upon belief in God. Are we seeking to think about people as he would have us think? Does our faith in God come into play when we face difficulty and trouble? Or is our belief in God only kept somewhere at the back of our minds while we take our own way?

The picture of the potter and the clay is a familiar image of God at work. We are the clay and he the potter. We must be as passive as the clay so that God can work his will in us and mould our lives to his design. Self- will, pride and ambition are fractious elements which thwart God's wisdom and love. Only when we realise our own sinfulness and inability to make anything good by ourselves, will we be soft enough and suppliant enough for God to shape us and use us.

Salvation begins at the point of despair, where we ask, 'What must we do to be saved?' There alone are we ready to listen to God and to open the door to his entry.

PRIVILEGE AND RESPONSIBILITY

Amos 3:1-3,8

¹Hear this word that the LORD has spoken against you, O people of Israel, against the whole family which I brought up out of the land of Egypt:

²"You only have I known
    of all the families of the earth;
  therefore I will punish you
    for all your inquities.

³"Do two walk together,
    unless they have made an ap-
      pointment?. ...

⁸The lion has roared;
    who will not fear?
  The LORD GOD has spoken;
    who can but prophesy?"

Never can any prophet's message have come to the Israelites with such a shock as this. In the previous chapters Amos has been pronouncing God's doom on other nations. Now he suddenly turns to Israel.

The Israelites looked on themselves as the 'chosen people'. They believed that God had no use for any other nation. The Gentiles, they said, were created to be fuel for the fires of hell. Further, they believed that they would receive preferential treatment from God. God would judge the other nations with one standard and the Jews with another. So Amos turns on them with God's message. 'You have I known of all the families of the earth. Just because of that, because you had more chances than anyone else, because your privileges were so much greater, your judgment will be harder and your punishment more terrible.'

Responsibility is always the other side of privilege. The more privileges a man has the greater his condemnation if he fails to live up to them. To have known God's truth and to have experienced God's love is a priceless privilege but also a heavy responsibility.

For meditation: *Have I a daily rendezvous with God?*

TRUE SERVICE OF GOD

Amos 5:4-7

> [4]For thus says the LORD to the house
>   of Israel:
>   "Seek me and live;
> [5]but do not seek Bethel,
>   and do not enter into Gilgal
>   or cross over to Beer-sheba;
>   for Gilgal shall surely go into exile,
>   and Bethel shall come to
>   naught."
>
> [6]Seek the LORD and live,
>   lest he break out like fire in the
>   house of Joseph,
>   and it devour, with none to
>   quench it for Bethel,
> [7]O you who turn justice to worm-
>   wood,
>   and cast down righteousness to
>   the earth!

Bethel was the place where the official worship of God was carried on — with sacrifices, elaborate forms of worship, and droves of priests. Amos declares that their elaborate paraphernalia of worship is irrelevant, and worse than irrelevant, because it is going on in the midst of social injustice, where the poor are oppressed and where men prey on each other.

Verses 8 and 9: God has created and upheld the universe with his immeasurable power and that power is there to avenge the humble man who has been the victim of greed and injustice.

No ritual, however elaborate, and no worship, however rich, can take the place of social justice based on love for our fellow men.

For reflection: *do I ever try to make the externals of religion a substitute for service to my fellows?*

THE DAY OF THE LORD

Amos 5:12-13, 18-20

> [12]For I know how many are your
> transgressions,
> and how great are your sins —
> you who afflict the righteous, who
> take a bribe,
> and turn aside the needy in the
> gate.
> [13]Therefore he who is prudent will
> keep silent in such a time;
> for it is an evil time. ...
> [18]Woe to you who desire the day of
> the LORD!
> Why would you have the day of
> the LORD?
> It is darkness, and not light;
> [19]as if a man fled from a lion,
> and a bear met him;
> or went into the house and leaned
> with his hand against the wall,
> and a serpent bit him.
> [20]Is not the day of the LORD darkness,
> and not light,
> and gloom with no brightness
> in it?

Amos came from the open hills and countryside. He enjoyed the simplicities of the life he had lived under the open sky. The life of the city shocked him to the core. At the gates of Jewish villages and cities there was a little place where the elders met and dispensed justice. But nowadays justice was dead and graft, bribery and corruption were supreme. The rich, instead of remembering their responsibilities to their poorer brothers, lived in ostentatious luxury. Amos was sure that all this injustice made a mockery of the elaborate worship that went on.

In verses 18-20 he attacks again. The Jews had a basic conception called 'The Day of the Lord.' They believed that on that day God would intervene in history to free them from all their troubles and make them masters of the world. They looked forward to the Day of the Lord as the day when all their selfish dreams would come true. Yes, Amos tells them, the Day of the Lord will come, but instead of being the day of glory, it will be a day of judgment, when those who should have known the right and who yet did the wrong will receive their punishment.

A prayer: *O God, help me to make my life such that I would be ready to welcome you at any moment.*

THE RIVER OF JUSTICE

Amos 5:21-7

[21]"I hate, I despise your feasts,
and I take no delight in your
solemn assemblies.
[22]Even though you offer me your
burnt offerings and cereal offerings,
I will not accept them,
and the peace offerings of your
fatted beasts
I will not look upon.
[23]Take away from me the noise of
your songs;
to the melody of your harps I
will not listen.
[24] But let justice roll down like waters,
and righteousness like an ever-
flowing stream.

[25]"Did you bring to me sacrifices and offerings the forty years
in the wilderness, O house of Israel? [26]You shall take up Sakkuth
your king, and Kaiwan your star-god, your images, which you made
for yourselves; [27]therefore I will take you into exile beyond
Damascus," says the LORD, whose name is the God of hosts.

It will assist our understanding of much of *Amos* if we remember
that in many cases the word *judgment* is used where modern English
would use the word *justice*. The dream of Amos, and, as he saw
it, the dream of God, is not a land where there is elaborate ritual
worship, but a land which is washed clean by a river of justice flowing through it.

The meaning of the two words Moloch and Chiun in verse 26
is very doubtful;* but they were probably both star gods. The ancient peoples believed that the stars could control a man's life and
destiny, and so they worshipped them. The fact that even today
people dabble in astrology and fortune-telling by the stars shows
how hard these ancient superstitions die. It is the complaint of Amos
that the people of Israel who should have known so much better
have fallen away from the worship of the true God to mere superstitions. That way, Amos is certain, lies ruin.

To think about: *do I allow superstition to have any part in my
life? Do I ever allow my conduct to be influenced by
superstitious beliefs?*

*Professor Barclay is referring to the *Authorised Version* of course. The correct reading is offered in the *RSV*, as given above.

THE MEASURING LINE OF GOD

Amos 7:1-9

[1]Thus the Lord GOD showed me: behold, he was forming locusts in the beginning of the shooting up of the latter growth; and lo, it was the latter growth after the king's mowings. [2]When they had finished eating the grass of the land, I said,

"O Lord GOD forgive, I beseech
thee!
How can Jacob stand?
He is so small!"

[3]The LORD repented concerning this;
"It shall not be," said the LORD.

[4]Thus the Lord GOD showed me: behold, the Lord GOD was calling for a judgment by fire, and it devoured the great deep and was eating up the land. [5]Then I said,

"O Lord GOD, cease, I beseech thee!
How can Jacob stand?
He is so small!"

[6]The LORD repented concerning this;
"This also shall not be," said the
Lord GOD.

[7]He showed me: behold, the LORD was standing beside a wallbuilt with a plumb line, with a plumb line in his hand. [8]And the LORD said to me, "Amos, what do you see?" And I said, "A plumb line." Then the Lord said,

"Behold, I am setting a plumb line
in the midst of my people Israel;
I will never again pass by them;

[9]the high places of Isaac shall be
made desolate,
and the sanctuaries of Israel shall
be laid waste,
and I will rise against the house
of Jerobo'am with the sword."

Verses 7-9: a plumb-line is a line with a weight on the endof it, and it is used to judge whether a wall or the side of a house is trueand vertical. So, says Amos, God will set his plumb-line in Israel to judgemen's lives.

There is one thought to which Amos returns again and again. He had a burning conviction that all the worship of the sanctuaries and the high places was nothing less than an insult to God when it was joined to a life and a civilisation where the very meaning of the word brotherhood had been forgotten and where there was no justice.

Sometimes Christianity is accused of being an other-worldly religion and of being so interested in heaven that it forgets the things of earth altogether.

THE DAUNTLESS PROPHET

Amos 7:10-17

[10]Then Amazi'ah the priest of Bethel sent to Jerobo'am king of Israel, saying, ''Amos has conspired against you in the midst of the house of Israel; the land is not able to bear all his words. [11]For thus Amos has said,

'Jerobo'am shall die by the sword,
and Israel must go into exile
away from his land.' ''

[12]And Amazi'ah said to Amos, ''O seer, go, flee away to the land of Judah, and eat bread there, and prophesy there; [13]but never again prophesy at Bethel, for it is the king's sanctuary, and it is a temple of the kingdom.''

[14]Then Amos answered Amazi'ah, ''I am no prophet, nor a prophet's son; but I am a herdsman, and a dresser of sycamore trees, [15]and the LORD took me from following the flock, and the LORD said to me, 'Go, prophesy to my people Israel.'

[16]''Now therefore hear the word of the
LORD.
You say, 'Do not prophesy against
Israel,
and do not preach against the
house of Isaac.'

[17]Therefore thus says the LORD:
'Your wife shall be a harlot in the
city,
and your sons and your daughters
shall fall by the sword,
and your land shall be parcelled
out by line;
you yourself shall die in an unclean
land,
and Israel shall surely go into
exile away from its land.' ''

Not unnaturally the official priests at Bethel resented this disturbing incomer and did their best to silence him.

Amos answered that he prophesied because God had laid his hand upon him and he could not help himself.

When Luther was threatened, he answered, 'Here I stand; I can do no other; so help me God.'

Amos and Luther show us two things. First, the source of truth. We shall only get the truth from God if we listen to his voice. Secondly, the source of courage. God never sent a vision to any man without the power to carry it out. To know that will bring courage to our faint hearts.

A prayer: *O God, help me to listen to your voice, and when you speak give me courage to obey.*

THE THREAT OF GOD

Amos 8:4-14

⁴Hear this, you who trample upon
    the needy,
      and bring the poor of the land
      to an end,
⁵saying, "When will the new moon
    be over,
      that we may sell grain?
    And the sabbath,
      that we may offer wheat for sale,
      that we may make the ephah small
      and the shekel great,
      and deal deceitfully with false
      balances,
⁶that we may buy the poor for silver
    and the needy for a pair of
    sandals,
    and sell the refuse of the wheat?"

⁷The LORD has sworn by the pride
    of Jacob:
    "Surely I will never forget any of
    their deeds.
⁸Shall not the land tremble on this
    account,
    and every one mourn who dwells
    in it,
    and all of it rise like the Nile,
    and be tossed about and sink
    again, like the Nile of Egypt?"

⁹"And on that day," says the Lord
    GOD,
    "I will make the sun go down at
    noon,
    and darken the earth in broad
    daylight.
¹⁰I will turn your feasts into mourn-
    ing,
    and all your songs into lamenta-
    tion;
    I will bring sackcloth upon all loins,
    and baldness on every head;
    I will make it like the mourning for
    an only son,
    and the end of it like a bitter day.

[11]"Behold, the days are coming,"
    says the Lord GOD,
    "when I will send a famine on
      the land;
    not a famine of bread, nor a thirst
      for water,
    but of hearing the words of the
      LORD.

[12]They shall wander from sea to sea,
    and from north to east;
    they shall run to and fro, to seek
      the word of the LORD,
    but they shall not find it.

[13]"In that day the fair virgins and the
      young men
    shall faint for thirst.
[14]Those who swear by Ash'imah of
      Samar'ia,
    and say, 'As thy god lives, O
      Dan,'
    and, 'As the way of Beer-sheba
      lives,'
    they shall fall, and never rise
      again."

See how practical Amos makes the nature of sin. These people falsified their balances and measures, and gave short weight; they debased the coinage and gave false value; they adulterated the wheat and gave inferior merchandise; they got the poor resourceless people into their power by lending on the pledge of their scanty possessions.

The real test of a man's religion is not whether he goes to church or reads his bible, or contributes money to the church funds. It is much more practical than that. If a man is a workman and an employee, is he a better, more diligent, more conscientious, more honest workman that the man who is not a Christian? If a man is a master and an employer, is he a fairer, juster, kinder, more generous employer, than the man who is not a Christian?

The insistence of the bible is that our religion, our faith, must be demonstrated in the ordinary activities of living. If we want to prove that Christianity is the best religion there is only one way to do it — to show that it produces the best men and women.

A prayer: *O God, help me so to live that men may see my good deeds and glorify you.*

THE GRACIOUS PROMISE

Amos 9:11-15

[11]"In that day I will raise up
the booth of David that is fallen
and repair its breaches,
and raise up its ruins,
and rebuild it as in the days of
old;
[14]I will restore the fortunes of my
people Israel,
and they shall rebuld the ruined
cities and inhabit them;
they shall plant vineyards and drink
their wine,
and they shall make gardens and
eat their fruit.
[15]I will plant them upon their land,
and they shall never again be
plucked up
out of the land which I have
given them,"
says the LORD your God.

This stern book finishes not with still another threat but with the loveliest of promises. From this we learn two things about the heart and mind of God.

God's punishment is never meant for the destruction of man but for his reformation. When a father punishes a child it is not that he finds pleasure in inflicting pain, but because he wants to make the child better.

It is so with God. When some trial comes to us, the first thing we should ask is, what is God meaning to teach me by this?

This passage also shows that God never gives up hope of men. To the end of the day he continues to believe in us. The people we love most of all are the people who know us at our worst and who still love us, whom we have disappointed sadly but who still trust us, who have forgiven us when we had no right to be forgiven. God is supremely like that.

A prayer: *O God, save me from ever using your love and patience as an excuse for sinning. Help me to be more worthy of the unfathomable, never-failing love which you have for me and for all mankind.*